SMART TESTS

Teacher-made Tests that Help Students Learn

C A T H E R I N E   W A L K E R

E D G A R   S C H M I D T

Pembroke Publishers Limited

We wish to acknowledge our friends and colleagues at Alberta Learning and Resource Development Services, Edmonton Public Schools for their on-going support, collaboration and contributions to this book.

© **2004 Pembroke Publishers**
538 Hood Road
Markham, Ontario, Canada L3R 3K9
www.pembrokepublishers.com

Distributed in the U.S. by Stenhouse Publishers
477 Congress Street
Portland, ME 04101-3451
www.stenhouse.com

We acknowledge the financial support of the Government of Canada through the Book Publishing Industry Development Program (BPIDP) for our publishing activities.

We acknowledge the Government of Ontario through the Ontario Media Development Corporation's Ontario Book Initiative.

National Library of Canada Cataloguing in Publication

Walker, Catherine (Catherine M.)
    Smart tests : teacher-made tests that help students
learn / Catherine Walker, Edgar Schmidt.

Includes index.
ISBN 1-55138-166-4

    1. Educational tests and measurements—Design and construction.
I. Schmidt, Edgar II. Title.

LB3060.65.W34 2004   371.26′1   C2003-907109-X

The following items are used or adapted with permission:

pages 30 (illustration), 99, 105, 109, 112 (BLMs): Antaya-Moore and Walker, *Smart Learning* (Alberta Learning, 2001); page 117 (illustration): *Make School Work for You* (Alberta Learning, 2001); page 119 (BLM): Chapman and King, *Test Success in the Brain-compatible Classroom* (Zephyr Press, 2000); pages 43, 49, 63, 69 (rubrics): *Thinking Tools for Kids* (Edmonton Public Schools, Resource Development Services, 1999); page 66 (rubric): *Think Again* (Edmonton Public Schools, Resource Development Services, 2003).

Editor: Kat Mototsune
Cover Design: John Zehethofer
Cover Photography: Photodisc
Typesetting: Jay Tee Graphics Ltd.

Printed and bound in Canada
9 8 7 6 5 4 3 2 1

Contents

Introduction

Paper-and-pencil tests created by teachers are the most common assessment tools used by elementary teachers. To be an important part of the learning and teaching process as well, these tests must be an integral part of daily classroom learning and instruction—not just the culminating event. Effective and fair tests give students opportunities to see their own progress, and give teachers information they need to decide how to best meet the learning needs of their students.

When compared to other performance tasks, paper-and-pencil tests can be the most efficient use of instructional and planning time, can be the easiest form to manage, and can generate the most tangible and easy-to-use data.

Smart tests are teacher-made tests that provide rich assessment information for making sound educational judgments about student learning. They are part of a balanced approach to assessment, which also includes focused instruction, relevant assignments, carefully selected performance-based assessments, thoughtful teacher observation, and appropriate standardized test data.

Classroom teachers know the learning needs of their own students and the context in which the students explore and apply specific skills and concepts. Therefore, they are the people in the best position to develop fair and effective tests for their students.

Well constructed and fairly administered teacher-made tests can provide evidence of quality learning and teaching. In this era of high-stakes accountability and the move to standardized testing, teachers' knowledge of and skill in assessing and making sound judgments is increasingly under scrutiny. A recent poll revealed that parents overwhelmingly favor teacher evaluation in assessing student achievement. To defend these judgments, teachers need strong and reliable evidence of student learning. The more sufficient the evidence, the more secure teachers, students, and parents can be in these judgments. Having the knowledge and skills to develop and carry out effective assessment practices—including teacher-made tests—returns the authority for measuring student learning to the classroom teacher.

In *Smart Tests*, we offer guidelines for effective test development and invite teachers to reflect on their own beliefs about tests. We provide information and strategies for developing tests for Grades 2 to 6, including suggestions on how to link thinking skills to tasks, how to use visual organizers, and how to create different types of questions. Many of the sample questions and assessment tasks are drawn from our own classroom experience. They illustrate how skills and concepts from different subject areas can be assessed and evaluated through thoughtful and engaging tasks across the grade levels. This bank of sample questions can serve as a model as you begin to develop your own bank of smart questions and tasks, and the samples are adaptable to any curriculum.

The process of assessment and evaluation doesn't start and stop with a single test. It begins the first day of the school year, infusing itself in daily classroom instruction and routines, and needs to be supported with a positive classroom climate. Teachers can help students prepare more effectively for tests by providing in-class reviews, teaching study skills and test-taking strategies, encouraging positive attitudes towards tests, and involving parents.

To this end, we include throughout the book three sets of specially designed tools to promote and support the planning, instruction, and assessment practices that help students become successful learners and thinkers. Teacher Tools encourage teachers to reflect and examine their own practices in test development and questioning. A set of visual organizers provides sample formats you can use to develop relevant and engaging assessment tasks. Student Tools provide structured opportunities for students to reflect on their own attitudes and work habits, including planning tools to help develop their own effective unit reviews and study plans. Home Tools provide parents with tips for helping their children prepare for tests, and for exploring and nurturing positive attitudes and work habits that will improve their children's success at school.

The goal of *Smart Tests* is to provide teachers with ideas and strategies for improving assessment practices and developing smart tests for Grades 2 to 6. Using better and smarter tests, you can engage and motivate the students in your classroom to become more successful learners and thinkers.

1

What Are Smart Tests?

The tests and other assessment tasks that individual teachers develop for their students communicate the teacher's beliefs about what skills, information, and concepts are important. Teachers demonstrate their commitment to encouraging students' higher-level thinking by creating assessment tasks that give students opportunities to apply new knowledge, reflect on their learning, defend opinions, and connect what they are learning to the world beyond the classroom. Moreover, tests are often the most visible evidence of student learning for parents to see and make judgments about. Each teacher-made test provides a revealing snapshot of what is happening in a classroom, and what knowledge, skills, concepts, and ways of knowing and doing the teacher values.

Guidelines for Smart Test Development

The work of instructing, assessing, and judging student learning is complex. Teachers' decisions have profound effects on students, and therefore decisions about how, when, and why to assess student learning must be thoughtful and confident. While large-scale standardized tests are the most obvious assessments, Stiggins points out that "they are not even in the same league as teachers' classroom assessments in terms of their direct impact on student well-being. Nearly all of the assessment events that take place in students' lives happen at the behest of their teachers.... Without question, teachers are the drivers of the assessment systems that determine the effectiveness of the schooling process" (Stiggins, pages 11–12). Smart tests can ensure teachers are driving in the right direction.

Unlike standardized tests, teacher-made tests are not intended to compare students to one another or provide a ranking of students within a class or across a grade level. A well developed teacher-made test is based on instruction, course content, and the skills and concepts in the unit of study. It provides a teacher with critical information to inform instruction, to provide feedback to students, and to make valid and fair judgments about student learning and performance. At each stage of the development and use of smart tests, consider the following guidelines.

Guidelines for Developing Assessment Tasks

- Match assessment tasks to the purpose and context of instruction. Tasks should relate directly to the goals of instruction and incorporate content and activities that have been part of the classroom instruction.
- Ensure tasks allow students to clearly demonstrate their knowledge, skills, and attitudes.

Guidelines for Collecting Assessment Information

- Make time for discussing with students both the purpose of specific assessment tasks and how the information these tasks generate can be used.
- Ensure students know how the assessment task will be scored and "what counts."
- Create safe and supportive learning environments that encourage all students to demonstrate their knowledge.
- Use assessment tasks that gather accurate and concrete information within reasonable time periods.
- Ensure that directions to students are clear, unambiguous, complete, and appropriate for the age, grade, and ability level of the students.
- If an unexpected event takes place during an assessment task, make a note of it and determine what affect, if any, it may have on the results.
- Modify or develop alternative assessment tasks for students with special needs, or those whose first language is not English.

Guidelines for Scoring Student Performance

- Before students perform the task, develop a scoring guide that considers the quality of the performance or product and the correctness of answers.
- Avoid scoring factors that are not relevant to the assessment purpose yet could influence the results. For example, if the critical factor in a writing task is content, then style choices should not affect scoring.
- Give students written feedback that will help them better understand the task and the related skills and concepts, so that they can improve their performance and enhance their learning.
- Be willing to change scoring procedures if there is a problem with the assessment tasks.
- Be willing to discuss and consider the opinions of students if they disagree with or do not understand their final test scores.

Guidelines for Interpreting and Reporting Assessment Information

- Weight individual tasks appropriately in order to make a summary judgment of the task.
- Grade effort, participation, work habits, and other behaviors that are not an explicit part of the unit skills and concepts separately, rather than as part of an achievement mark.

- Include the identification of student strengths and areas for improvement as part of the reporting of assessment results.

Explore Your Beliefs about Testing

To explore your own beliefs about teacher-made tests, complete the questionnaire on pages 10–11. There are no right or wrong answers for these questions. Rather, they reflect a continuum of attitudes towards tests and testing, and provide an opportunity to explore and reflect where you are on that continuum. Clarifying what you believe also gives you information and insights to adjust your own instruction and assessment practices, so they more closely align with you believe.

A brief discussion for each questionnaire item follows. Like all good learning and teaching activities, this discussion of possible responses may generate more questions than it actually answers! For most items, the smart-test theory explored in this book tends to the "agree" end of the continuum, but often there are valid arguments for both ends of the scale. Teachers need to work through each issue and identify what they find is right and appropriate for their own practice in their own classrooms. It might also be an interesting exercise to complete the questionnaire again after reading the book, to see if your beliefs and attitudes toward testing have shifted after trying some of the strategies.

Using Teacher Tool #1: What Do You Believe about Tests?

1. Teachers should provide an in-class review for all tests.
In-class reviews tend to create a more level playing field for students and make it more possible for all students in the class to perform well on assessment tasks. An effective review will ensure that students clearly understand what material will be on the test, what tasks might look like, and what kind of strategies they can use for review. (For more on in-class reviews see Chapter 2, Chapter 5, and Chapter 6.)

2. Teachers should provide study plans for major tests.
An effective study plan, particularly in the elementary grades, ensures that tests are an integrated part of classroom instruction. By developing study plans with students, you model strategies that can become part of students' learning repertoire throughout the grades. (For more on study plans, see Chapter 6.)

3. Teachers should provide test questions ahead of time.
Test questions and assessment tasks should be similar, in both format and content, to those used during regular classroom instruction throughout the school year. Whenever possible, sample questions and tasks should also be part of the review process. This creates opportunities for students to practise demonstrating their learning within these specific contexts. Knowing what kind of questions to expect, and what content will be covered on the test, reduces the element of surprise and gives students a better opportunity to prepare. (For more on using questions in instruction, see Chapter 5.)

Teacher Tool #1

What Do You Believe about Tests?

Use these questions to reflect on your assessment practices. Decide whether you agree, disagree, or are undecided.

1. Teachers should provide an in-class review for all tests.
   ❏ agree   ❏ disagree   ❏ undecided

2. Teachers should provide study plans for major tests.
   ❏ agree   ❏ disagree   ❏ undecided

3. Teachers should provide test questions ahead of time.
   ❏ agree   ❏ disagree   ❏ undecided

4. Students need a minimum of three days to prepare for major tests.
   ❏ agree   ❏ disagree   ❏ undecided

5. Several small tests are more valuable than one major test.
   ❏ agree   ❏ disagree   ❏ undecided

6. Multiple-choice assessment tasks provide a more objective assessment than short-answer assessment tasks.
   ❏ agree   ❏ disagree   ❏ undecided

7. Teachers should audiotape tests for less-able readers.
   ❏ agree   ❏ disagree   ❏ undecided

8. Teachers should be willing to clarify directions during tests.
   ❏ agree   ❏ disagree   ❏ undecided

9. Test questions should extend beyond the essential skills and concepts in a unit of study.
   ❏ agree   ❏ disagree   ❏ undecided

10. Tests should be time-limited.
   ❏ agree   ❏ disagree   ❏ undecided

11. Test anxiety negatively affects learning.
    ❏ agree   ❏ disagree   ❏ undecided

12. Students should correct their own tests.
    ❏ agree   ❏ disagree   ❏ undecided

13. Incorrect spelling should affect test scores.
    ❏ agree   ❏ disagree   ❏ undecided

14. Any test items that all students get wrong should be discounted.
    ❏ agree   ❏ disagree   ❏ undecided

15. Any test items that all students get right should be discounted.
    ❏ agree   ❏ disagree   ❏ undecided

16. Students should be able to rewrite tests.
    ❏ agree   ❏ disagree   ❏ undecided

On the other hand, giving students exact test questions ahead of time may encourage rote memorization. If students rely on memorization, the assessment task will provide less useful data about student learning than if they rely on understanding. It will not provide a true picture of how students can apply and synthesize new skills and concepts.

4. Students need a minimum of three days to prepare for major tests.
Since major tests often include material covered over a period of weeks or even months, it makes sense to allow students more than one day to organize material and review skills and concepts. Research identifies the optimal study schedule to deepen understanding of new learning as brief, frequent, and intense periods of 20 to 30 minutes, over several days. (For more on scheduling tests, see Chapter 5.)

5. Several small tests are more valuable than one major test.
Multiple assessment tasks provide a richer source of data for interpreting assessment than a single test can.

However, learning new skills and concepts takes time, as does integrating new knowledge with prior learning. Testing too frequently or using too many learning activities as assessment tasks can limit the available exploration and practice time that is vital to student learning. It also takes time to develop quality assessment tasks, organize in-class review, and develop study plans for major tests.

Consider focusing on quality over quantity by limiting the number of major tests and scheduling them at strategic points throughout the school year.

6. Multiple-choice assessment tasks provide a more objective assessment than short-answer assessment tasks.
Multiple-choice assessment tasks are easier to score than other types and, because responses are either right or wrong, there will be consistent scoring from one marker to the next.

However, fair and valid multiple-choice assessment tasks are challenging and time-consuming to develop. Because of the narrow constraints of this question format, it is easy to develop multiple-choice tasks that are invalid, fail to measure understanding of a specific skill or concept, or are contrived or misleading. For some students, multiple-choice response tasks are not congruent with how they think and learn; if multiple-choice tasks are the only type of assessment tasks used to assess their learning, these students will not have a fair opportunity to show what they know.

A smart test provides students with various ways to demonstrate their learning. This could involve several multiple-choice tasks in combination with short-answer and other types of questions and assessment tasks. (For more on developing effective multiple-choice questions see Chapter 2; for more on developing types of test questions, see Chapter 2, Chapter 4, and Chapter 5.)

7. Teachers should audiotape tests for less-able readers.

Fair assessment tasks create opportunities for all students, including those who are less-able readers, to demonstrate their mastery of skills and concepts. If reading the assessment task is a barrier to demonstrating what certain students know, it may be necessary to make accommodations or adaptations to ensure these students have the support they need to demonstrate their learning. Unless the assessment task is specifically assessing reading abilities, success on the assessment task should be dependent on a student's understanding and mastery of the specific learner outcomes being tested, not on reading ability.

Making audiotapes of major tests might be an appropriate accommodation for individual students, particularly if they will be using a similar adaptation for standardized tests. Occasional verbal prompts from the teacher may be all some students need, while others may require a designated reader. Accommodations used during assessments should be a regular part of the learning and teaching routine throughout the school year. (For more on accommodating the needs of individual students, see Chapter 7.)

8. Teachers should be willing to clarify directions during tests.

Weak reading skills should not be a barrier to students' ability to demonstrate their learning in the content areas. Unless the assessment task is explicitly measuring independent reading skills, you should be willing to provide assistance to individual students who need some clarification of directions during a test.

When more than one student asks for clarification on a particular set of directions, it may indicate that the directions are unclear. In the interest of fairness, be proactive and clarify those directions to the whole class, rather than assisting only the individual students who ask.

When clarifying directions, be careful not to add new information or provide clues, particularly if not all students will be receiving the clarification. Giving too much information to students during an assessment task lessens the effectiveness of the assessment and limits the amount and depth of valid information the assessment will generate. (For more on clarifying directions, see Chapter 6.)

9. Test questions should extend beyond the essential skills and concepts in a unit of study.

Asking a question that requires knowledge and understanding extending beyond the essential skills and concepts of a unit may provide information about an individual student's knowledge and skills.

However, this information should not affect an achievement mark for that grade level and subject area. Consider the analogy of people applying for a license to drive a car being asked to demonstrate their proficiency driving a school bus or an airplane; being able to drive a school bus or airplane might be important skills, but they are not prerequisite or essential to driving a car. Assessment tasks used to measure grade-level achievement should relate, and be limited, to the specific skills and concepts for that particular unit of study or grade level. (For more on matching skills and concepts to assessment tasks, see Chapter 2.)

10. Tests should be time-limited.

Time-limited tests provide information on how quickly students can process information and develop responses. If speed is an important aspect of a specific skill, then it may be appropriate to consider limiting the time available for the related assessment task.

If the only purpose of the time limit is to differentiate high-ranking students from lower-ranking ones, then time limits are not a valid part of a fair test.

When students require significantly long periods of time to complete tasks, you need to discuss this issue during the reporting process. (For more on helping students manage their time, see Chapter 7.)

11. Test anxiety negatively affects learning.

Although a little anxiety, or positive stress, can actually heighten concentration and enhance performance, it is important to balance high standards with the anxiety and feelings of discouragement or failure that interfere with a student's ability to demonstrate learning. Test anxiety can be a real problem for a small but significant number of students. When students are excessively anxious, they are not able to communicate their understanding, knowledge, and skills effectively. Adequate preparation, such as in-class reviews, study plans, and supportive testing environments, can go a long way toward alleviating students' negative feelings about tests and learning. (For more on managing test anxiety, see Chapter 6.)

12. Students should correct their own tests.

Students need to be involved in assessing and evaluating their own learning. For some tests, it might be appropriate for students to correct their own test papers under the guidance of the teacher. Whether or not students are involved in the initial scoring of their own tests, they should have an opportunity to review and discuss their responses at some point in the learning process. This will give them feedback on their performance and opportunities to correct incomplete or incorrect responses.

By listening to other students sharing sample responses and discussing how they arrived at their answers, students will learn new strategies and ways of thinking to enhance their own performance on future assessment tasks. (For more on student self-reflection, see Chapter 8.)

13. Incorrect spelling should affect test scores.

Unless the explicit purpose of an assessment task is to assess students' spelling skills, incorrect spelling should not affect whether a response is scored as correct or incorrect.

If individual students have such weak spelling skills that it is difficult to interpret their written responses, then these students need appropriate interventions and accommodations. Strategies such as using an electronic spell-check or reviewing written responses aloud with a teacher will ensure that these students have fair opportunity to demonstrate their true understanding and mastery of skills and concepts being assessed. (For more on spelling difficulties on tests, see Chapter 7.)

14. Any test items that all students get wrong should be discounted.
Developers of standardized tests avoid or eliminate tasks that all students get wrong because they not useful for ranking students.

If specific assessment tasks cause difficulty for all students in the class, revisit the task to find out what the problem is. It could be a poorly developed assessment task, or it might identify skills and concepts that the whole class did not master. It may indicate that the whole class would benefit from further instruction and different learning activities related to these skills and concepts. (For more on test difficulty, see Chapter 2.)

15. Any test items that all students get right should be discounted.
Developers of standardized tests avoid or eliminate tasks that all students get right because these tasks do not help them rank students.

It is a time for celebration when all students earn full marks on a specific task on a teacher-made test! It is evidence that the teacher's instruction is working and students are learning. (For more on test difficulty, see Chapter 2.)

16. Students should be able to rewrite tests.
The underlying goal of assessment should always be to encourage student learning, not to discourage it. Giving students opportunities to review tests they did not do well on and to demonstrate their learning creates what Guskey describes as the second chance "[that] helps determine the effectiveness of the corrective instruction and offers students another opportunity to experience success in learning." (Guskey, page 10)

2

Developing Smart Tests

The ideal time to create a test is during the planning of the unit, before instruction begins. Begin the test development process with the end in mind.

Identify Learner Outcomes

The first step in successful test development is to identify the essential skills and concepts in the unit of study. Establishing clear goals and clearly articulating what you want students to be able to do for each unit test focuses the test development process. Sharing these goals with students will help them prepare for tests.

Sample goal for Grade 6 Social Studies unit test on local government	This test will give students opportunities to demonstrate their knowledge of local government structures and the roles they play in our community. Students will demonstrate their understanding of how they, as citizens, can influence local government decisions. The test will count for 35 percent of the term mark.

To develop goals for specific tests, ask the following questions about a unit of study:

- What do students need to know?
- What do students need to be able to think about?
- What do students need to demonstrate?

It may not always be necessary to assess every skill and concept in a unit of study on a test. Selecting only the most essential skills and concepts for a test ensures that the most important elements of the unit are assessed. By identifying essential outcomes early in the unit plan, you can develop learning activities that ensure students acquire the experiences and practice they need to successfully master the outcomes.

Consider Thinking Skills

To build assessment tasks for tests, match each skill or concept with a type of question or performance task that will create the best opportunities for students to demonstrate their understanding.

Bloom's taxonomy (below) offers a basic framework for generating a variety and range of assessment tasks. This range of question types can provide students opportunities to answer questions at various levels of thinking. It can generate rich assessment information, not only about what students know, but also what additional learning they need. Consider the definitions, sample cue words, and sample tasks and products in the following table.

Bloom's Taxonomy

	Definition	Sample Cue Words	Sample Tasks/ Products
Evaluation and **Synthesis** are parallel thinking skills.			
Evaluation	Judge something according to specific criteria or standards.	discuss, decide, rank, justify, select, debate, assess, prove, recommend	decision, rating, editorial, debate, position paper
Synthesis	Combine information to create new knowledge or concepts.	compose, invent, design, generalize, propose alternatives, create, forecast	action plan, invention, proposal, design, ad, poem, story
Analysis	Examine facts in separate parts to see how they relate to each other or how they are unique; understand structure and motive; identify fallacies.	identify parts, compare and contrast, classify, analyze, sort and group, arrange, examine, identify relationship between, identify what is wrong, provide evidence	compare-and-contrast chart, survey, report
Application	Use information in new situations or to solve problems.	demonstrate use, solve a problem, predict	action plan, prediction
Comprehension	Use facts and knowledge to demonstrate basic understanding of concepts and skills.	give examples, explain how facts are related, summarize or restate in your own words	summary, examples
Knowledge	Recall and recognize facts.	name, list, record, show, select, match, find, describe, identify, outline, label	definition, matched terms, labelled diagram, list

The following examples show how specific skills and concepts can be developed into a variety of assessment tasks that use different levels of thinking.

Sample questions using range of thinking skills

Learning Outcomes	Sample Questions
Grade 2 Science Compare the amount of liquid absorbed by different materials.	**Recall** Which of the three kinds of paper we tested was most absorbent? **Comprehension/ Application** Write three questions you could ask a person who makes paper for a living about how different types of paper are made. **Evaluation** Of the three kinds of paper we tested, which one would be best for building a paper boat? Tell why you picked that paper.
Grade 6 Science Identify adaptations that enable birds and insects to fly.	**Recall/ Comprehension** Name five features of a bird's body that enable it to fly. **Application** A bird has been brought to a bird sanctuary, unable to fly. It is normally a strong flyer. List five reasons the bird might not be able to fly, and explain how each of these reasons could affect the bird's flight. **Evaluation/ Synthesis** Compare and contrast the flight of hawk with the flight of a bee. Describe their similarities and differences in flight. Which one would be best suited to making quick turns and stops? Explain how physical adaptations allow it to do this.

Create Good Test Questions

Building strong assessment tasks requires careful thinking about what it is you want students to demonstrate during the test. The questions must relate to skills and concepts in the unit of study and provide students with opportunities to demonstrate what they know. Equally important is the interpretation of test scores. Think about how you can demonstrate how you make your judgments. Communicating this to students and parents will create opportunities for understanding, reflection, and improved learning.

What Makes a Good Assessment Task?

Test items for standardized tests are field tested with large groups of students in order to determine their validity and reliability. Validity means that the test actually measures what it says it measures. Reliability, at its simplest, means that test results are consistent from one group of students to another. Fairness, validity, and reliability are important concepts for teacher-made tests because the more valid and reliable the assessment task, the more sound the judgments about student learning will be.

Fair Questions

Fair questions

- are based on skills and concepts that students have explored and practised in class, and are relevant to the unit of study.
- use language and formats similar to those that were used in class instruction.
- are sensitive to the experiences and values of various groups of students in the class and the school. If members of specific groups perform better (or worse) on certain test questions, then a bias may be present. For example, if a question relies on background knowledge that can be only acquired at home, such as cooking with a parent or traveling as a family to other places, students who spend time in the kitchen with a parent or from families with the economic means to travel will have an advantage over others. Watch for these kinds of biases that may affect certain social, ethnic, or gender groups.
- avoid using special language, playing on words, or adding irrelevant information not related to the skills and concepts being assessed.

Valid Questions

There are two steps to creating valid tests: developing valid questions and interpreting test results fairly. Valid test questions will tend to lead to valid test interpretations.

- Ensure that the content of each task is relevant and representative of skills and concepts in the unit of study.
- Ensure that tasks include process and content questions related to essential concepts of the unit. Identify the thinking skills students must use to successfully complete the assessment task.
- Use language and question types that students have experience with.
- Ensure that both language and complexity of questions are appropriate for students' grade and ability level.
- Be sure the range of questions covers content and processes adequately. Under-representing essential skills and concepts reduces test validity.
- Be sure that the questions do not include irrelevant items that make the questions either too easy or too difficult.

Reliable Questions

Question reliability is the relationship between the questions and the group of students taking the test. When different student groups who have had similar instruction perform more or less consistently on a set of tasks or questions, those questions and tasks are considered reliable.

Reliability improves when several questions are developed to test a specific set of concepts. The more questions, the more chances for reliability. This is why a single longer test is often considered more reliable than a number of shorter quiz-type tests.

Common Formats

Varying question and test formats gives students richer opportunities to demonstrate their knowledge and skills.

Matching Tasks

Matching items provides students with opportunities to link related concepts or vocabulary. The simplest format is the term-and-definition matching question, which is usually of the knowledge or recall type. You can extend the thinking involved in answering these types of questions by including extra terms that don't have matching definitions, and challenging students to write their own definitions for these terms.

Sample assessment task from a Grade 3 Math test

Draw lines between the matching number sentences.

4 x 3	2 x 10
4 x 4	4 x 9
6 x 6	2 x 6
4 x 5	2 x 8

Sample assessment task from a Grade 5 Language Arts test

Match each of the characters from *Jeremy Thatcher Dragon Hatcher* with the three words or phrases that best describes his or her character.

Jeremy Thatcher	trusting, affectionate, good communicator
Mary Lou Hutton	lonely, animal lover, curious
Hyacinth Priest	book lover, mysterious, trustworthy
Tiamat	lonely, high standards, book lover
Mr. Kravitz	animal lover, trustworthy, artistic

Now, write your own three describing words that match Spress's character:

Short-answer Questions

Short-answer questions require students to articulate key understandings in a few sentences. They challenge students to produce responses rather than simply recognizing a correct answer. Short-answer questions need to contain enough information and directions so that students clearly understand what they are being asked to do.

Sample assessment task from a Grade 3 Math test	John found five coins in the pocket of his winter coat. He counted the money and he had 46¢. What five coins did John find in his pocket?
Sample assessment task from a Grade 5 Language Arts test	(on Bruce Coville's *Jeremy Thatcher Dragon Hatcher*) Did the dragon trust Jeremy? What did the story say that made you believe that?

Fill in the Blanks

This type of task requires students to place missing words in a few sentences or a paragraph. Key vocabulary words related to the outcomes have been left out of the passage, and students must comprehend the passage and apply the correct terms. A variation of this type of question includes providing a separate box containing the entire vocabulary needed to fill in the blanks.

Sample assessment task from a Grade 2 Science test	Use the words **hotter** or **colder** to correctly complete each sentence. 1. Hot chocolate is _____ than milk. 2. Winter is _____ than summer. 3. An ice cube is _____ than water. 4. The sun is _____ than the Earth. 5. A snowman is _____ than a swimming pool.
Sample assessment task from a Grade 6 Science test	Fill in the correct word for each statement. 1. _____ trees lose their leaves in the fall. (Answer: *deciduous* or *hardwood*) Evergreen or _____ trees keep their leaves throughout all of the seasons. (Answer: *coniferous*) 2. Plants give off _____ and take in _____ during the process of photosynthesis. (Answers: *oxygen, carbon dioxide*)

Essay Questions

Essay questions give students opportunities to expand on multiple and complex concepts. They challenge students to produce arguments and evidence for their point-of-view or conclusion, and demand high-level planning and thinking. Essays may be confined to narrowly defined topics requiring students to respond in a limited way, or they may be more open-ended, giving students latitude to compose their own responses. A well developed essay question requires both careful planning of the essay topic and a comprehensive scoring guide that both teachers and students can use.

Sample assessment task from a Grade 4 Language Arts test

The novel *Jeremy Thatcher Dragon Hatcher* has won several awards. What makes it a good book that young people enjoy reading? Give at least three convincing reasons why other students might like this book. Be sure to include your own reaction to the story, explaining what your favorite part of the book was and why you found it especially interesting or meaningful. Your goal in writing this book review is to get a person reading your review to run to the library or bookstore and get this book!

Before you begin writing, read over the following rubric so you understand how your essay will be marked.

4 Standard of excellence	3 Exceeds acceptable standard	2 Acceptable standard	1 Needs improvement to meet acceptable standard
CONTENT			
❏ Makes clear and insightful observations about story, character, and theme	❏ Makes clear and detailed observations about story, character, and theme	❏ Makes general observations about story, character, and theme	❏ Makes vague or inaccurate observations about story, character, and theme
❏ Analyzes favorite part of story and describes personal reactions and connections to the story	❏ Describes favorite part of story and explains why	❏ Identifies favorite part of story and states why	❏ Mentions favorite part of story
❏ Successfully convinces reader that this book is worth reading	❏ Strong attempt to convince reader that this book is worth reading	❏ Basic attempt to convince reader that this book is worth reading	❏ No attempt to convince reader that this book is worth reading

4	3	2	1
Standard of excellence	Exceeds acceptable standard	Acceptable standard	Needs improvement to meet acceptable standard
WRITING CONVENTIONS			
❏ Shares the purpose and sets the tone for essay with opening sentence that captures attention of reader	❏ States purpose and sets tone for essay with interesting opening sentence	❏ States purpose of essay in opening sentence	❏ Weak opening sentence does not tell purpose of essay
❏ Uses words and phrases to create interesting language throughout essay	❏ Uses interesting and precise words throughout essay	❏ Uses interesting words throughout essay	❏ Uses vague wording with minimal description
❏ Uses skillful grammar, correct spelling, and word choice that adds to reader's enjoyment of essay	❏ Uses correct spelling and grammar that enhances quality of essay	❏ Uses correct spelling and grammar so essay is easy to read and understand	❏ Spelling and grammar errors interfere with meaning and readability

Sample assessment task from Grade 6 Social Studies test

You and a few of your friends love skateboarding and believe there should be a public skateboarding park for young people in your community. Who would you need to convince that this is a real need? Think about would you need to tell that person about

- what you want
- why you want it
- why it's important for your community
- how people will benefit
- how this project could be done.

Now, write a convincing letter to that person outlining the need for a public skateboarding park in your community.

Before you begin writing, read over the following rubric so you understand how your essay will be marked.

4	3	2	1
Standard of excellence	Exceeds acceptable standard	Meets acceptable standard	Needs improvement to meet acceptable standard
❏ Opens letter with convincing statement of purpose that captures reader interest	❏ Clearly states purpose of letter and gets reader's attention	❏ States purpose of letter in opening sentences	❏ Purpose of letter is vague
❏ Presents convincing facts and intriguing ideas to support point of view	❏ Presents detailed facts and interesting ideas to support point of view	❏ Presents facts and ideas to support point of view	❏ Facts and ideas are vague
❏ Provides a precise and analytic description of why this issue is important and how the community can benefit	❏ Clearly explains why this issue is important and how the community can benefit	❏ States why this issue is important	❏ Offers a vague or weak explanation of why this issue is important and what the benefits might be
❏ Offers convincing plan that could influence others to change their thinking or opinions and fully support this proposal	❏ Offers interesting ideas that could help others consider this point of view	❏ Offers ideas for what needs to happen in order for this proposal to begin	❏ Ideas for making proposal happen are vague or not plausible

Multiple-choice Questions

Multiple-choice questions require students to select the correct answer from three or four answers presented. Answering these types of questions successfully requires students to think about the question stem and then determine the most correct response from among other options, called *distractors*. Developing good multiple-choice questions is time consuming and requires creativity.

- Provide one response that is absolutely correct, or is clearly the best choice, and make sure that all distractors have an element of plausibility.
- Use positively phrased stems and put as much information as possible in the stem. Try to make the stem so complete that students can use it to guess the approximate answer before reading the possible responses.
- Avoid repetition of key words in the correct response.
- Make sure all distractors are parallel in construction and grammatically sound.

- Avoid using throw-away distractors such as "all of the above" or "none of the above."

Begin with simple questions that give students opportunities to apply knowledge.

Sample assessment task from a Grade 2 Science test

Amanda put two bottles of water on the shelf. One had a lid and the other did not. The next day she noticed that

a. the bottle with no lid had more water than the bottle with the lid.
b. the bottle with the lid had less water than the bottle without the lid.
c. the bottle with no lid had less water than the bottle with the lid.
d. the bottle with the lid was empty.

Use dialogues, diagrams, or scenarios to create two or more questions that explore attitudes and issues. A smart test uses a variety of question formats. Clustering a combination of question formats around a scenario helps students focus their thinking on a few key concepts at one time.

Sample assessment task from a Grade 6 Social Studies test

Use the speakers' comments below to answer the following three questions.

"Girls didn't need to go to school in ancient Athens. They could learn everything they need to at home from their mothers. I think they had good lives, they were free to enjoy good food and their beautiful homes."
— Nik, a Grade 6 student.

"The goddesses of ancient Greece were considered powerful and the people worshipped them. But the ordinary women were not treated as well. If they couldn't pick their own husbands, take part in government, or even go out in public, they might as well have been slaves."
— Amanda, a Grade 6 student

1. The main issue being discussed by Amanda and Nik is whether or not
A. people should worship goddesses.
B. women need the right to go out in public.
C. women need the right to make choices about their lives.
D. women need the right to marry young.

Nik believes that girls in ancient Athens had advantages because
A. they didn't have to go to school.
B. their rights were protected.
C. they had beautiful homes.
D. they married young.

Amanda believes that women need to
A. be worshipped.
B. be protected.
C. participate fully in society.
D. be educated at home.

True-or-false Questions

True/false questions require students to decide whether or not a specific state-ment is correct. These types of questions concentrate on specific and narrow concepts that can be reduced to absolute terms. Older students can be challenged to explain why a statement is either true or false.

Sample assessment task from a Grade 2 Science test	Insects have eight legs.	❏ true	❏ false
	Insects have five body parts.	❏ true	❏ false
	Insects hatch eggs.	❏ true	❏ false
	All insects can fly.	❏ true	❏ false

Sample assessment task from a Grade 6 Social Studies test

Explain why each of the following statements is NOT true.

A. Men and women did NOT meet at the town centre to discuss important matters in ancient Athens because _____

_____ .

B. Ancient Athenian citizens did NOT elect representatives to debate issues and vote on decisions for them. Instead _____

_____ .

C. It was NOT dangerous for soldiers to travel between city-states during the ancient Olympic Games because _____

_____ .

Better Test Questions

Writing effective tests is challenging and time consuming. Analyze assessment tasks and questions in existing tests and look for ways they can be revised to cre-ate better opportunities for your students to demonstrate their knowledge and understanding. Consider the following questions and how they were revised.

Basic Test Questions	Better Test Questions
In this story, what color is the dog?	*What makes the dog's color important in this story?*
This question calls for simple recall, asking students to locate and repeat the fact in the story.	Students are required to recognize not only the dog's color, but to determine how it is important in relation to other aspects of the story.
Match each term with the correct definition.	*Match each term with the correct definition. When you are finished the matching there will be three terms left over. Write your own definition for each of these terms.*
Students are required to simply recognize the correct answer.	In addition to demonstrating recognition of terms, students have an opportunity to construct their own definition of three terms.

Basic Test Questions	Better Test Questions
Label the map, identifying cities and the rivers that run through them. Students are required to recall city and river names and match them appropriately.	*Label the map, identifying cities and the rivers that run through them. Select one city and provide three reasons why the river is important to that city.* Students are required to identify relationships between cities and rivers, as well as compose a rationale for their positions.
Write true or false after each statement. Students are required to recognize a correct response.	*Write true or false after each statement. If the statement is false, rewrite it to make it true.* Students are required to recognize correct responses and to apply their knowledge to explain why certain statements are not true.

To create better assessment tasks, consider the range of thinking skills that can be used to complete the tasks. Creating activities and tasks that demand higher levels of thinking, during both instruction and assessment, provides richer evidence for assessing and evaluating student learning and progress.

How Difficult Should Tests Be?

Developers of standardized tests are concerned with differentiating or discriminating between achievement levels. They try to ensure that each test has a small range of questions that prove difficult even for the most capable students, and a set of questions answerable by most students. Questions that are correctly answered by all students are often eliminated for scoring. It is not necessary or appropriate to apply these scoring strategies to teacher-made tests, as these kinds of tests are not intended to discriminate between different students—the primary goal is to find out what each student knows and understands in relation to the skills and concepts of that particular unit of study.

Maintaining an appropriate level of difficulty in a teacher-made test is a balancing act. Teachers need to ensure that the test has a balance of basic-level questions and challenging ones, and that all tasks relate directly to specific skills and concepts in the unit. If tests are too difficult in the elementary grades and do not create opportunities for students to be successful, students may become discouraged and will have a more difficult time connecting how their effort in test review and preparation contributes to their achievement mark.

Decide What Counts

Deciding the value of individual assessment tasks is an important consideration when scoring tests. Consider the following factors when assigning numerical values to individual assessment tasks.

One Response, One Mark

If test questions have one correct and unequivocal answer, then the question should be worth one mark. This would be the case for multiple-choice, true/false, and matching questions. For short-answer or essay questions, a predetermined number of facts or processes will guide the number of marks assigned for the question. For example, a score of five might include five accurate and related facts, or one position statement with at least four logical reasons.

Instructional Time

Generally, the more time spent on instruction of a specific learning outcome, the more weight it will have on the test and in the overall assessment plans for a unit of study. However, if certain skills require remedial instruction and use an inordinate proportion of instruction time, these skills should not be unduly emphasized on a single test.

Complexity of Concepts and Related Tasks

Tasks requiring higher levels of thinking should carry more weight than tasks requiring a less complex response, such as a definition or labeling a diagram.

Number of Questions or Tasks

The total number of questions or tasks on a test affects the weighting of specific skills and concepts. Having more questions on a specific concept will naturally give it more weight. Because it may be easier to generate questions for specific concepts or skills, ensure that the number of questions related to each concept or skill does not skew marks toward ones that are less important.

Consistent Scoring on Open-ended Tasks

Scoring short-answer and essay questions can be challenging because students will respond in a variety of ways. Before you begin scoring open-ended tasks, it is important that you have a clear understanding of the basic elements needed to demonstrate limited, basic, or superior understanding. A scoring guide, such as the four-point scale on page 29, can be a useful tool when scoring these questions. The scoring guide not only keeps scoring consistent among a set of questions; it can also provide useful feedback to students and parents.

Four-Point Scale for Scoring

0 – No knowledge or understanding
No response or a completely incorrect response that conveys no understanding of the skill or concept.

1 – Limited knowledge and understanding
The response shows limited knowledge or understanding of the skill or concept and the response is fragmented and difficult to interpret.

2 – Basic knowledge and understanding
The response conveys basic understanding of the skill or concept.

3 – Superior knowledge and understanding
The response is a completely correct answer and conveys detailed and extended understanding of the skill or concept.

Build in Extra Support

There are a number of simple ways you can build in extra support as you design tests for elementary students. Look for ways of asking and formatting questions that give students opportunities to be as successful as possible.

Provide Words of Encouragement

Use encouraging words in the directions at the beginning and end of test. For added emphasis, illustrate encouraging words with speech balloons or other graphics. Choose your words carefully—emphasize effort (versus luck) and remind students to actively encourage themselves throughout the test.

> "Welcome to the Grade 6 Science test. This is your opportunity to show all that you learned during the Flight unit."

> "We had a lot of fun and worked very hard on the Wheels and Levers unit. Now is your chance to show what a wheels and level expert you are! Read all the questions carefully and think back to the activities and discussion we had in class…"

Remind students to use encouraging self-talk throughout the test.

At the end of the test, take the opportunity to reinforce students' efforts with an encouraging note

> "You've finished your test—give yourself a pat on the back. Now read back over each test question to make sure your answers show all that you know."

Encourage Goal Setting

Use the beginning of the test as an opportunity for students to set goals for how they intend to perform on the test.

Sample student test goal	My goal for this test is to earn a mark of _____ .
	I prepared for this test by _____ .

Adjust Reading Level

Keep sentences short and to the point. Use familiar words in both the directions and the questions. Be as concrete as possible. If it is necessary to use terminology that some students may struggle with, provide more familiar word in brackets or within the same sentence.

Make the Format Easy to Use

Students need organized formats for demonstrating their knowledge and understanding. Make sure the tests you create for your students have ample space and easy-to-use formats for recording information and ideas. Consider including simple charts and other familiar graphic organizers for students to use. Include headings that provide additional guidance for successfully completing the task. Create sufficient white space between each question and use a large, clear font. If tasks have a number of components, use simple numbering and lettering systems to help students stay organized.

Sample assessment task from a Grade 5 Social Studies test

Compare and contrast the lives of typical families from one of the Aboriginal groups we have studied. Consider what their lives might have been like in each of the three different time periods.

Name of Aboriginal group: _____

	Before European contact (c. 1550)	1750–1850	2000
A. Family life			
B. Food			
C. Homes			
D. Community organization			
E. Work			
F. (Make up your own category)			

Reinforce Directions

Use **bold** or *italic* type to emphasize important words in directions and questions. Use familiar language and, when possible, include at least one sample response so students are sure what type of answer they need to be looking for.

Sample assessment task from a Grade 5 Science test

There was a note at the scene of the crime. It had been a while since Henry analyzed handwriting so he made himself a list of things to look for. Help Henry complete his list. The first one is done for you.

> What to look for in forgeries:
> 1. *crossing of t's* _____
> 2. _____
> 3. _____
> 4. _____
> 5. _____
> 6. _____

Offer Hints when Asking for Explanations

Sometimes a simple hint will kick-start students' responses and encourage them to extend their thinking. A well placed hint can build confidence and help uncover and retrieve learning and understanding. Hints can be delivered by thought balloons with prompts and questions, illustrations, or subject headings.

Sample assessment task from a Grade 6 Science test

Why is a rocket shaped like a pencil but this satellite is shaped like a ball?

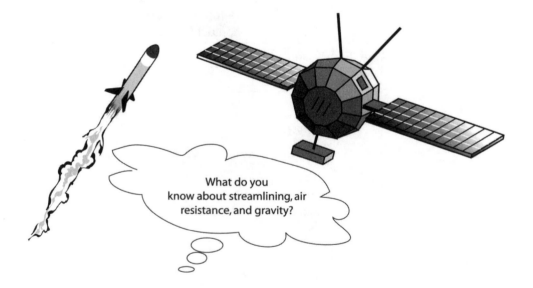

What do you know about streamlining, air resistance, and gravity?

Add Memory Cues

Create tasks that do not over-rely on memorizing specific lists or categories. This kind of memory-reliant task can interfere with students' ability to demonstrate their understanding of certain concepts. For example, a student might understand rules of a certain game but not be able to remember all the categories of rules. Providing the categories frees the student up to concentrate on the higher-level task of demonstrating their understanding of the game.

Sample assessment task from a Grade 4 Physical Education test	In your own words, explain five important rules of inter-lacrosse. A. Contact _____ _____ _____ B. Moving with the ball _____ _____ _____ C. Trapping the ball _____ _____ _____ D. The key _____ _____ _____ E. Referee _____ _____ _____

Link Two Kinds of Information

Sometimes it may be helpful to provide one piece of relevant information to help students access their knowledge of a related concept.

Sample assessment task from a Grade 6 Social Studies test	China was isolated from the rest of the world for many centuries. List the physical features of this country that helped keep it separated from its neighbors. A. _____ B. _____ C. _____

Make Tasks Personally Relevant

Look for creative ways to make the test personally relevant to students. Consider using names of children in the class in questions and scenarios. Make references to familiar and favorite class and school activities. When appropriate, cluster a number of questions around one engaging scenario and, if possible, include a graphic. This will provide motivation and enhance meaning for many students.

Sample assessment task for a Grade 3 Math test

Alison and Alex are in charge of the class Halloween party.

They want to do six different activities at the party and they will have one hour for the whole party. Make a schedule for the party showing how long the class will do each of the six activities.

Ms. Jones made 30 cupcakes for the party. There are 23 students in the class. How many extra cupcakes will there be?

There are 18 girls in the class and half of them plan to come to the party as superheroes. None of the boys plan to dress as superheroes. How many superheroes will be at the party?

Reflect and Review

Student Self-reflection

Give students opportunities to reflect on their own learning and their performance on tests. The information about what students know and how they think can be valuable to teachers and parents. A student self-reflection page, such as Student Tool #1 on page 35, could be attached as the last page of a test.

Reviewing Tests with Students

A unit of instruction is not complete just because the unit test has been completed. It is important to bring students back to reflect on what they have learned and what they need to improve upon so that they might be better prepared for the next test.

Reflecting on My Test

Name: _____   Date:_____

1. I understood all the questions.
   ❏ absolutely!   ❏ yes   ❏ not really   ❏ no

2. I did my best thinking on every question.
   ❏ absolutely!   ❏ yes   ❏ not really   ❏ no

3. I had enough time to finish the test.
   ❏ absolutely!   ❏ yes   ❏ not really   ❏ no

4. I remember learning these topics during class.
   ❏ absolutely!   ❏ yes   ❏ not really   ❏ no

5. The way the questions were asked helped me show what I know.
   ❏ absolutely!   ❏ yes   ❏ not really   ❏ no

6. A. The questions that were the easiest for me were…

   B. These questions were easy because…

7. A. The question that was the most difficult was…

   B. This question was difficult because…

8. What surprised me most about this test was…

9. To prepare for my next test I will…

Find a way to review tests that works with your students. Consider doing a test review as a group activity: have students make corrections on their own tests as the answers are discussed and recorded on an overhead transparency or the chalk board. Invite individual students to provide answers to the questions. When there is more than one possible response to a question, discuss the variations and the factors to consider when making the choice.

Older students may be able to work independently and use their notebooks and textbooks to make corrections and improvements to their answers. Corrections for a unit test can become a separate assignment, and its score can be calculated into the unit mark.

Teacher Self-reflection

Building smart tests is an ongoing process that relies on thoughtful reflection at all stages: as you are planning tests, after the students have completed the test, and after you have reviewed the test results with students and their parents.

Use Teacher Tool #3: Checklist for Smart Test Development on page 37 to assess the process you are using to develop tests to assess student learning in your classroom.

Continue assessing your own progress by asking yourself reflective questions after you have administered and scored a major test.

- Did the test allow me to make valid judgements about what students know and are able to do?
- Were there any basic skills and concepts for which students showed a much higher or lower level of understanding and mastery than I predicted?
- Which thinking skills did students demonstrate proficiency with? Which thinking skills did they have more difficulty with?
- Were there any tasks or questions for which a specific group of students did poorly?
- Did the question formats work?
- Did the students clearly understand the questions?
- Did the test take a reasonable amount of time to complete?
- Were the accommodations for students with special needs effective?
- How did the student reflections help in understanding learning and levels of performance?
- What other kinds of information do the test results provide?

Collaborate With Other Teachers

Developing smart tests takes time, skill, and effort. It requires knowledge of curriculum and subject areas, a strong understanding of assessment principles and an ability to solve problems creatively. Individual teachers can develop smart tests on their own, but collaborating with another teacher—or better yet, a small group of committed colleagues—can be an effective and efficient way to improve assessment practices in your school. Share sample questions and assessment tasks across the subject areas. Build on skills and concepts from grade to grade. Talk about how the instructional process can influence assessment, and how assessment can

Checklist for Smart Test Development

1. I developed the first draft of the test as part of the planning process before teaching the unit. ❏ yes ❏ not yet

2. Each question on the test is clearly aligned with specific skills and concepts from the unit of study. ❏ yes ❏ not yet

3. Each type of question will be familiar to the students because it was introduced and practised through regular classroom instruction this school year. ❏ yes ❏ not yet

4. The directions for each section of the test are clear. ❏ yes ❏ not yet

5. The point value is written beside each question on the test. ❏ yes ❏ not yet

6. There are at least three types of questions on the test. ❏ yes ❏ not yet

7. Question types are grouped together. ❏ yes ❏ not yet

8. The layout of the test is easy to read and there is ample space for students to record answers. ❏ yes ❏ not yet

9. The reading level is appropriate for this group of students. ❏ yes ❏ not yet

10. At least half of the test items encourage higher-level thinking. ❏ yes ❏ not yet

11. This test can be completed within one hour. ❏ yes ❏ not yet

12. I have included modifications so students with special needs can successfully demonstrate their learning on this test. ❏ yes ❏ not yet

13. Students have an opportunity to reflect and communicate on the quality of their work. ❏ yes ❏ not yet

influence instruction. Work collaboratively to develop criteria and exemplars for specific tasks that students will be doing on major tests. Opportunities to discuss standards and share strategies for engaging students help create a learning community in your school.

3

Using Visual Organizers

Visual organizers (also called thinking tools, graphic organizers, or key visuals) are formats for organizing information and ideas graphically. They use words, pictures, and graphic cues to help students generate ideas, record and reorganize information, and see relationships. A number of visual organizers can be used across the grade levels and across subject areas. Many of these interactive tools are multi-purpose and encourage the use of multiple levels of thinking skills.

Used as assessment tasks, visual organizers

- can act as windows into students' understanding and thinking. They can demonstrate not only *what* students are thinking, but also *how* they are thinking as they work through specific learning tasks.
- can be used to ask students to do familiar tasks with new material or new tasks with familiar material.
- can be used to create short assessment tasks on tests. Students can use the information in the organizer to ask another question, or they can complete a section of an organizer that has incomplete information.
- can be supplied as part of the assessment task, or can be designed by students with experience using related organizers to fit the task.
- can include a rubric listing the scoring criteria, so students are aware of the standards, and so that teachers can score the test objectively, consistently, and efficiently.

Visual organizers, either used to supply information for or on a test, or created by the student as part of a test, have practical advantages as assessment tasks.

- They require less time to complete than traditional essay questions.
- They can be successfully completed by students who do not have strong organizational and/or writing skills and may not be able to communicate their understanding of a concept through traditional essay formats.
- They provide cues for students so they understand clearly what the task is and what they are being asked to do. They can help students focus on the task by creating a supportive structure for students to use to show what they know.

- Visual organizers allow teachers to modify assessment procedures for individual students. A customized visual organizer can give students with special needs the extra structure and support they need to be successful. Other tools can be modified to challenge and encourage creativity and divergent thinking for students who need more of a challenge.
- If a rubric accompanies visual organizer tasks, the job of assessing the task will be easier and the scoring will be more objective and consistent.

For a visual organizer to be fair as an assessment task, it should have been introduced in the regular instructional program and students should have experience using it in a variety of situations. Like any assessment task, directions for a task using a visual organizer need to be clear and explicit. Students need to know

- how much information they need to include (e.g., three to five points in each column of a T-chart)
- what type of information they need (e.g., from your own experience, from the story, or from what you learned in the science unit)
- how much detail they need to include (e.g., key words, brief descriptions, complete sentences.)

The following ten organizers are examples of the types of tools that can be adapted as assessment tasks. Each tool has potential for assessing different levels of thinking; checked boxes indicate which skills could be assessed with a task designed around a specific visual organizer. Sample curriculum-related assessment tasks and scoring rubrics are also included for each type of organizer.

Venn Diagrams

☑ Knowledge ☑ Comprehension ☐ Application
☑ Analysis ☐ Synthesis ☐ Evaluation

A Venn diagram (see Teacher Tool #4, page 41) is made up of a set of two or more interlocking circles that provide space for comparing and contrasting information about two or more concepts or things. By breaking a concept into similar and dissimilar characteristics, students are able to think about and work with more complex issues. This comparing and contrasting format creates a process they can use to analyze in a systematic way.

Some students may work better on a more linear version of a Venn diagram, such as a compare and contrast chart (see Teacher Tool #5, page 42).

Visual Organizer: Venn Diagram

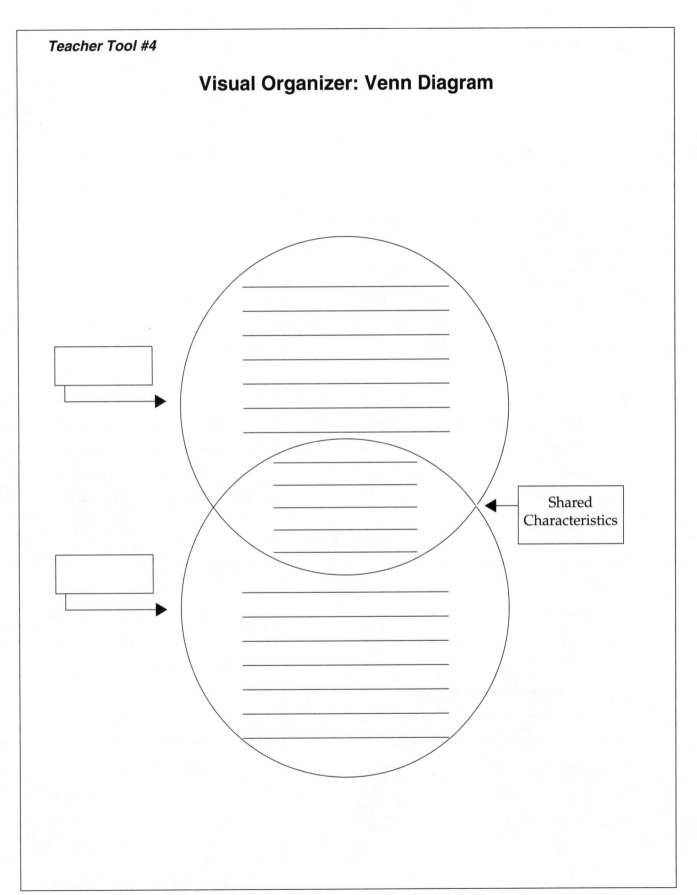

Shared Characteristics

Visual Organizer: Venn Chart

_____

Similarities

_____

_____

_____

_____

_____

_____

_____

Differences

_____   _____

_____   _____

_____   _____

_____   _____

_____   _____

_____   _____

_____   _____

Scoring Rubric for a Venn Diagram

4 (Standard of excellence)

- identifies many attributes that two concepts share
- identifies many ways that concepts are different from one another
- uses precise, detailed vocabulary to describe attributes
- information contains thought-provoking detail
- uses subheads to logically sequence and cluster information
- clearly and creatively labels all parts of the diagram
- has a descriptive and attention-getting title

3 (Exceeds acceptable standard)

- identifies several attributes that two concepts share
- identifies several ways that concepts are different from one another
- uses descriptive vocabulary to describe attributes
- information contains interesting details
- uses subheads to indicate sequence of information
- clearly labels all parts of the diagram
- has a descriptive title

2 (Meets acceptable standard)

- identifies some attributes that two concepts share
- identifies some ways that concepts are different from one another
- uses appropriate vocabulary to describe attributes
- information contains essential detail
- organizes information
- labels main parts of the diagram
- has an appropriate title

1 (Needs improvement to meet acceptable standard)

- identifies few or incorrect attributes that two concepts share
- identifies few or incorrect ways that concepts are different from one another
- uses vocabulary to describe attributes that is vague and/or is incorrect
- information is missing essential detail
- there is a minimal attempt to organize information
- labels of diagram are incomplete
- has a missing or incomplete title

Sample assessment tasks using Venn Diagrams	• Write all the factors that make up each number: 12, 54. Now, place the factors common to both numbers in the centre of the Venn diagram and place the remaining factors that belong with the number in the outer circles. What do you notice about the common factors of 12 and 54? • Compare and contrast the physical geography of Alberta and Quebec. Use a Venn diagram to show how they are the same and how they are different. • What important characteristics did the two major characters in this novel share? How were they different from one another? Use a Venn diagram to demonstrate your understanding of these two characters.
Sample of completed Venn Diagram	On the lines below, write all the factors that make up that number. 12: *1, 12, 2, 6, 3, 4* 54: *1, 54, 2, 27, 6, 9, 3, 18* Now, place the factors common to both numbers in the centre of the diagram and place the remaining factors that belong with the number in the outer circles

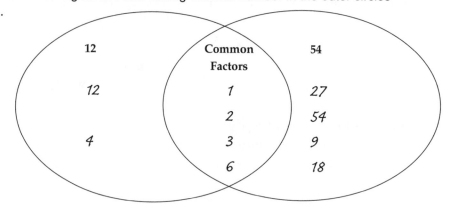

What do you notice about the common factors of 12 and 54?

I noted that both numbers can be divided in half equally and that the common factors are multiples of 2 and 3.

I also think 1 is a common factor of all numbers.

See page 43 for the scoring rubric.

Top-ten Lists

☑ Knowledge   ☑ Comprehension   ☑ Application
☑ Analysis   ☑ Synthesis   ☐ Evaluation

Made popular by television and radio, top-ten lists (see page 45) challenge students to come up with ten related strategies, reasons, or examples, and encourage students to think more deeply, broadly, and creatively about a specific topic. These lists can personalize learning and reflection, and at the same time encourage students to consider ideas beyond their immediate experience.

Top Ten List

The Top 10

_____

1._____

2._____

3._____

4._____

5._____

6._____

7._____

8._____

9._____

10._____

Scoring Rubric for a Top-ten List

4 (Standard of excellence)

- identifies multiple convincing and unexpected reasons, examples, or strategies
- uses precise, detailed vocabulary

3 (Exceeds acceptable standard)

- identifies multiple convincing reasons, examples, or strategies
- uses descriptive vocabulary

2 (Meets acceptable standard)

- identifies a number of appropriate reasons, examples, or strategies
- uses appropriate vocabulary

1 (Needs improvement to meet acceptable standard)

- identifies reasons, examples, or strategies that are erroneous or inappropriate
- uses vocabulary that is vague and/or incorrect

Developing a top-ten list can go beyond simple recall tasks when students are challenged to demonstrate higher levels of thinking; they can use the list as an opportunity to create their own examples and show they comprehend specific concepts and can apply new knowledge. These tasks can become acts of synthesis—putting thoughts together to create something new.

Generating possibilities is a crucial first step in decision making and problem solving. Students' lists of generated ideas can demonstrate their insight into situations, and how broadly and deeply they can think about a specific subject.

Sample assessment tasks using Top-ten Lists	• Make a top-ten list of reasons why daily physical activity is important to your health. • Use a top-ten list to create a convincing argument of why reading is better than watching television. • Make a top-ten list of how cities and towns encourage citizen participation in local government. Be creative and include some ideas for what cities and towns may not be doing right now but should consider doing in the near future.
Sample of completed Top-ten Lists	Top 10 Reasons for Daily Physical Activity: 1. *Gives you more energy* 2. *Stretches your muscles* 3. *Clears your head so you can be a better thinker* 4. *Helps you maintain a healthy weight* 5. *Helps build a stronger heart and lungs* 6. *You learn and practise new skills like running and jumping* 7. *Relieves stress* 8. *Focuses you on looking after your body and your health* 9. *Becomes a healthy habit for life* 10. *Is fun!*

See page 46 for the scoring rubric.

Discussion Webs

☐ Knowledge ☑ Comprehension ☑ Application
☑ Analysis ☑ Synthesis ☑ Evaluation

Discussion webs (see Teacher Tool #9, page 48) are frameworks for looking at two sides of a single issue, event, or decision. They can be useful tools for assessing students' understanding of literature because they encourage students to identify evidence in the text that supports their conclusion about characters, events, or themes the work.

Visual Organizer: Discussion Web

Two-Sided Disussion

Question

YES ◄ · ► NO

And my conclusion is

_____

_____.

I think this because

_____

_____.

Scoring Rubric for a Discussion Web

4 (Standard of excellence)

- clearly identifies issue with vivid description that could motivate reader to explore issue
- objectively and creatively explores different points of view
- develops detailed and convincing arguments for both sides of the issue
- identifies own conclusion and provides convincing and detailed rationale for choice
- information is accurate, detailed, well-organized, and presented with clarity

3 (Exceeds acceptable standard)

- clearly identifies issue with interesting description that could encourage reader to explore issue
- objectively explores different points of view
- develops convincing arguments for both sides of this issue
- identifies own conclusion and provides detailed rationale for choice
- information is accurate and organized

2 (Meets acceptable standard)

- identifies basic issue
- explores different points of view
- develops basic arguments for both sides of this issue
- identifies own conclusion and provides rationale for choice
- information is accurate

1(Needs improved to meet acceptable standard)

- issue is vaguely or incorrectly identified
- has only minimal attempt to explore different points of view
- basic arguments are incomplete and/or incorrect
- identifies own conclusion but does not explain rationale
- information is inaccurate, vague, or missing

Discussion webs are a form of decision making—deciding what to do when a choice has to be made. Skillful decision making involves blending a range of different types of thinking skills, including skills at generating ideas, clarifying ideas, sequencing ideas, and assessing the reasonableness of ideas.

Sample assessment tasks using Discussion Webs	• Complete a discussion web that investigates an important decision made by a character in the novel study.
	• Use a discussion web to explore whether bylaws to restrict smoking in public places will reduce the number of young people who start smoking.
	• Should voting in a federal election be a legal obligation? Use a discussion web to show both sides of this issue.

Sample of completed Discussion Web	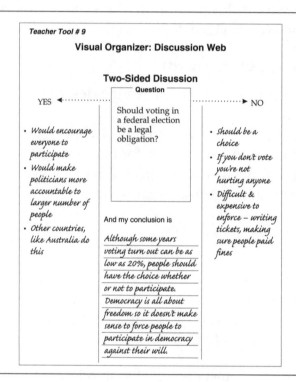

See page 49 for the scoring rubric.

Multiple Perspectives Frameworks

☑ Knowledge   ☑ Comprehension   ☐ Application
☑ Analysis   ☐ Synthesis   ☐ Evaluation

Multiple perspective frameworks (see Teacher Tool #11, page 51) create a format for identifying and recording multiple perspectives on a single issue. These tools use word bubbles, boxes, or thought balloons to illustrate how different people can have different feelings, positions, and view points on the same issue. The various perspectives can be supplied as part of the instructions or format of the assessment task; or identifying potential stakeholders who might have differing perspectives could be part of what students have to do to complete the task.

Multiple Perspectives

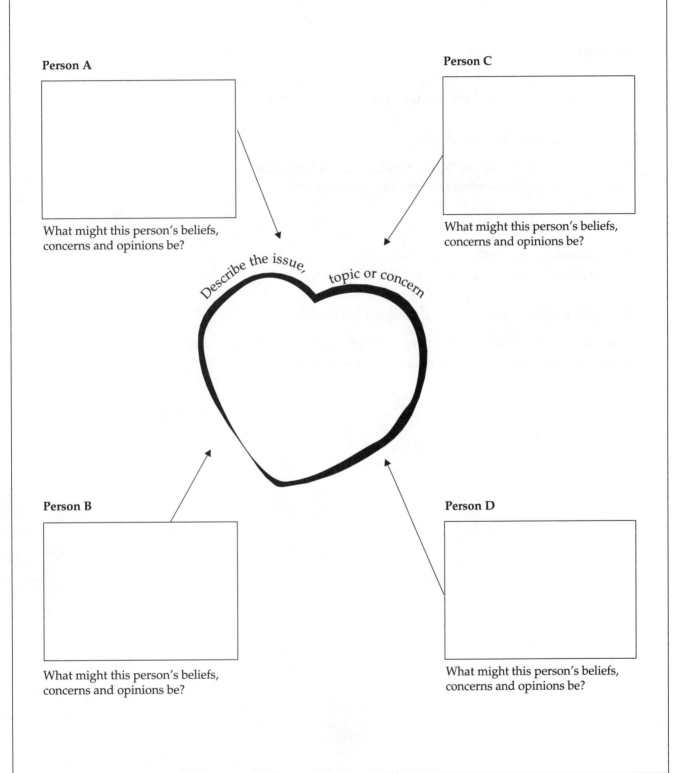

Person A

What might this person's beliefs, concerns and opinions be?

Person C

What might this person's beliefs, concerns and opinions be?

Describe the issue, topic or concern

Person B

What might this person's beliefs, concerns and opinions be?

Person D

What might this person's beliefs, concerns and opinions be?

Scoring Rubric for a Multiple Perspectives Organizer

4 (Standard of excellence)

- identifies convincing and thought-provoking perspectives for each viewpoint
- uses precise, detailed vocabulary for each perspective

3 (Exceeds acceptable standard)

- identifies convincing perspectives for each viewpoint
- uses descriptive vocabulary for each perspective

2 (Meets acceptable standard)

- identifies appropriate perspectives for each viewpoint
- uses appropriate vocabulary for each perspective

1 (Needs improvement to meet acceptable standard)

- identifies erroneous or inappropriate perspectives for each viewpoint
- uses vocabulary that is vague and/or incorrect

Students need encouragement to go beyond stereotypical responses and develop each stakeholder argument as authentically, as convincingly, and with as much empathy as possible. As well as for exploring different sides of a single issue, this tool can be used to explore and demonstrate understanding of specific events, character, and themes in short stories and novels.

Sample assessment tasks using Multiple Perspectives

- Forest fires are a great concern for people. Some people believe it is a good idea to let forest fires burn out rather than spend large amounts of money to fight them if they are 100 kilometres or more away from cities and towns. Consider the perspectives of each of these people, and whether they would agree or disagree with this idea: firefighter, wildlife officer, cottage owner, lumber company, environmentalist, someone or something else that might be affected by the fire.
- Describe the experience of participating in the art show from the perspective of four different characters in the novel.
- How did Canadian society view Emily Carr's art during her lifetime? Identify at least four different groups of people who would know about her art and use the word balloons to record what they thought of her work and why they believed this.

Sample of completed Multiple Perspectives organizer

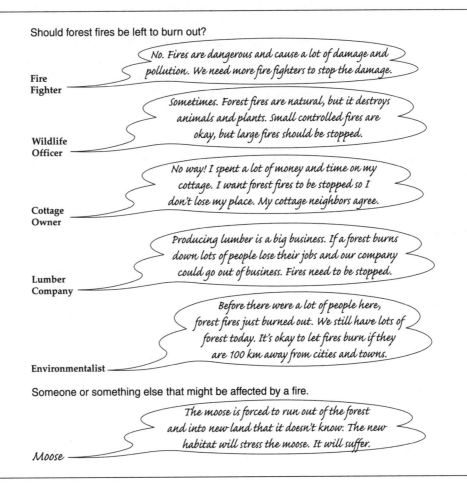

Should forest fires be left to burn out?

Fire Fighter: *No. Fires are dangerous and cause a lot of damage and pollution. We need more fire fighters to stop the damage.*

Wildlife Officer: *Sometimes. Forest fires are natural, but it destroys animals and plants. Small controlled fires are okay, but large fires should be stopped.*

Cottage Owner: *No way! I spent a lot of money and time on my cottage. I want forest fires to be stopped so I don't lose my place. My cottage neighbors agree.*

Lumber Company: *Producing lumber is a big business. If a forest burns down lots of people lose their jobs and our company could go out of business. Fires need to be stopped.*

Environmentalist: *Before there were a lot of people here, forest fires just burned out. We still have lots of forest today. It's okay to let fires burn if they are 100 km away from cities and towns.*

Someone or something else that might be affected by a fire.

Moose: *The moose is forced to run out of the forest and into new land that it doesn't know. The new habitat will stress the moose. It will suffer.*

See page 52 for the scoring rubric.

Webs

☑ Knowledge ☑ Comprehension ☑ Application
☑ Analysis ☑ Synthesis ☑ Evaluation

Webs are tools for generating new ideas, recording ideas about a particular topic, or showing relationships between different ideas. Different kinds of webs provide different levels of organization. The web gets its name from the way information is organized on the tool—single words or phrases are connected to other words the way the individual threads of a spider's web are all connected. This visual organizer helps students show how supporting data is related to the central idea.

Webs can take a number of different formats, depending on the type of information being webbed, how the information will be used, and the learning style of the person creating and using the web.

Webs have the potential to be used a number of different ways as assessment tasks. Students could be asked to complete one or more sections in a web. For example, in a web based on the 5-W's Plus Two (see Teacher Tool #13, page 55), students could demonstrate their understanding of a particular story or event by completed the Why?, How?, and Now What? parts of an existing web.

Webs can be also used to create short-answer assessment tasks in which students identify correct and incorrect information on a completed web.

Interpreting webs can also be a focus of an assessment task. A web on the test can supply information that students use to complete a number of related multiple-choice or short-answer tasks.

Sample assessment tasks using Webs

- Use a web to show all the ways you could use to prepare for an important test.
- Draw a web to show the important elements of the story.
- Make a web showing all that you know about how animals get ready for winter.

Sample of completed Web

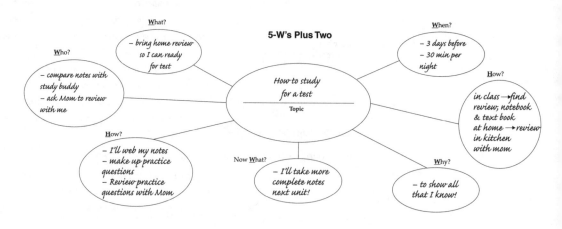

See page 56 for the scoring rubric.

Web

5-W's Plus Two

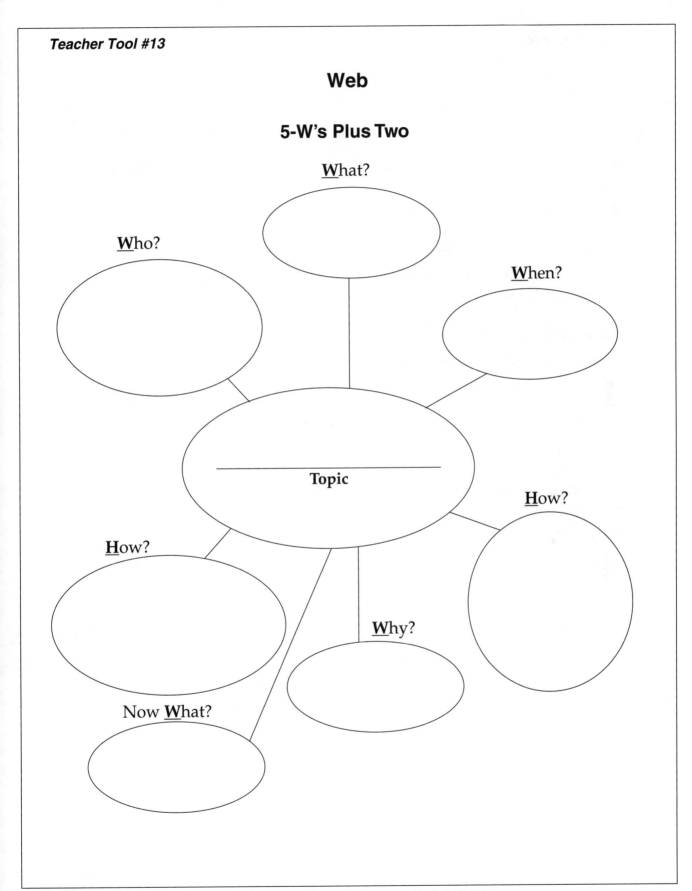

Scoring Rubric for a Web

4 (Standard of excellence)

- presents convincing and unexpected reasons, examples, strategies, or information in each category
- uses precise, detailed vocabulary

3 (Exceeds acceptable standard)

- presents convincing reasons, examples, strategies, or information in each category
- uses descriptive vocabulary

2 (Meets acceptable standard)

- presents appropriate reasons, examples, strategies, or information in each category
- uses appropriate vocabulary

1 (Needs improvement to meet acceptable standard)

- presents reasons, examples, strategies, or information that are erroneous or inappropriate
- uses vocabulary that is vague and/or incorrect

P-M-I Charts

☑ Knowledge   ☑ Comprehension   ☑ Application
☑ Analysis   ☑ Synthesis   ☑ Evaluation

A P-M-I chart (see Teacher Tool #15, page 58) is a tool for listing the Plus, Minus, and Interesting aspects of a particular issue or choice. P-M-I charts help students generate ideas and organize information. They also create a framework for making informed decisions. In addition to the three columns for listing the plus, minus, and interesting, a summary box can be added and customized to encourage students to use the information in the P-M-I columns to create a summary statement or make a decision.

Sample assessment tasks using a P-M-I Chart

- Do a P-M-I chart about living in a rural North American community and decide whether or not you would like to grow up in a rural community.
- Use a P-M-I chart to evaluate the quality of the structure you built for your science project. Use the summary box to explain how you would change the structure if you were to build it again.
- Think about the main character's experience in the bike race. Use the summary box to explain whether or not you think the race was worth the effort. What feelings and experiences of rider support your decision?

Sample of completed P-M-I Chart

Was the race worth the effort?

Plus	Minus	Interesting
He felt strong and confident at the start. He learned to keep going and not give up. He made some new friends at the end.	In the middle of the race, he felt weak and he wanted to give up. He didn't think it was worth it. He felt lonely and worried.	When he saw that he was not being passed by others anymore, he began to think that he could finish the race.

Was it worth the effort? What feelings and experiences of the rider support your decision?

He was really scared in the middle. He thought he would fail. When he saw that he was keeping up with the others, he wanted to keep going. It was hard work but it was worth it because he made new friends.

See page 59 for the scoring rubric.

P-M-I Chart

Topic/Issue _____

_____

Plus[+]   Minus[−]   Interesting[*]

_____   _____   _____
_____   _____   _____
_____   _____   _____
_____   _____   _____
_____   _____   _____
_____   _____   _____

And now I think

_____

_____

because _____

_____

Scoring Rubric for a P-M-I Chart

4 (Standard of excellence)

- develops detailed and convincing observations for each of the three categories
- identifies own conclusion and provides convincing and detailed rationale for choice
- information is accurate, detailed, well-organized, and presented with clarity

3 (Exceeds acceptable standard)

- develops convincing observations for each of the three categories
- identifies own conclusion and provides detailed rationale for choice
- information is accurate and organized

2 (Meets acceptable standard)

- develops basic observations for each of the three categories
- identifies own conclusion and provides rationale for choice
- information is accurate

1 (Needs improved to meet acceptable standard)

- observations are incomplete and/or incorrect
- identifies own conclusion but does not explain rationale
- information is inaccurate, vague, or missing

Flow Charts

☑ Knowledge   ☑ Comprehension   ☑ Application
☐ Analysis   ☐ Synthesis   ☐ Evaluation

A flow chart is a tool for investigating or explaining a process. Showing the relationship between steps and the sequence of steps in a process, flow charts can be clearer and more concise than written text. They can be used to define, explain, or summarize a process, present a set of instructions, or show changes (or cause and effect) over time. They can be helpful when students are demonstrating their understanding of a process in nature or the causes and effects of a historical event.

Effective flow charts have

- one step per box or panel
- concise and precise text
- accurate pictures, often with labels
- a good match between words and pictures
- arrows to show sequence and/or relationships.

A linear flow chart (see Teacher Tool #17, page 61) is a sequence of words and images joined by arrows. It is generally uses a format of numbered panels.

A cyclical flow chart (see Teacher Tool #18, page 62) can be used to illustrate continuous or renewable processes.

Sample assessment tasks using Flow Charts

- Draw a flow chart showing how a seed grows into a flower.
- Use four panels of a flow chart to show how the milk we drink for breakfast everyday gets to our kitchen table.
- Show what you could do if another student on the playground tried to bully you. Draw a picture of each step on your flow chart and use key words to explain what you could say and do.
- Use a cyclical flow chart to show how you can use addition to check if a subtraction question is correct. Use words and a number example to show the process.

Sample of completed Flow Chart

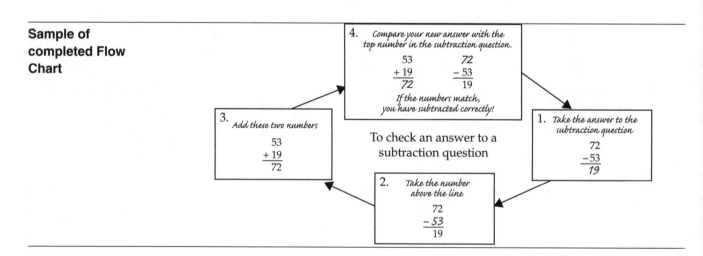

See page 63 for the scoring rubric.

Linear Flow Chart

Title: _____

Cyclical Flow Chart

Topic: _____

```
                    ┌─────────────────┐
                    │ 4.              │
                    │                 │
                    │                 │
                    │                 │
                    └─────────────────┘
          ┌─────────────────┐     ┌─────────────────┐
          │ 3.              │     │ 1.              │
          │                 │     │                 │
          │                 │     │                 │
          │                 │     │                 │
          └─────────────────┘     └─────────────────┘
                    ┌─────────────────┐
                    │ 2.              │
                    │                 │
                    │                 │
                    │                 │
                    └─────────────────┘
```

Scoring Rubric for a Flow Chart

4 (Standard of excellence)

- uses accurate, detailed diagrams and key words to illustrate process or concept
- uses precise and detailed vocabulary to enhance illustration of process or concept
- detailed information is correctly sequenced with relationships between events clearly visible
- includes detailed information that shows sophisticated understanding of process or concept

3 (Exceeds acceptable standard)

- uses accurate diagrams and key words to illustrate process or concept
- uses precise vocabulary to enhance illustration of process or concept
- information is correctly sequenced with relationships between events clearly visible
- includes detailed information that shows strong understanding of process or concept

2 (Meets acceptable standard)

- uses basic diagrams and key words to illustrate process or concept
- uses appropriate vocabulary to support illustration of process or concept
- information is correctly sequenced
- includes information that shows basic understanding of process or concept

1 (Needs improvement to meet acceptable standard)

- diagrams and key words are confusing, incorrect, or incomplete
- uses vague or incorrect vocabulary to support illustration of process or concept
- information is out of sequence and/or disorganized
- information shows weak understanding of process or concept

Problem-solving Models

☐ Knowledge   ☑ Comprehension   ☑ Application
☑ Analysis   ☑ Synthesis   ☐ Evaluation

Problem-solving models (see Teacher Tool #20, page 65) create frameworks for students to work through a step-by-step process of

- identifying a problem
- generating potential solutions
- choosing the best solution
- developing an action plan
- setting criteria for knowing whether the solution was successful or not.

Problem-solving models can be customized to accommodate different learning situations. For older students, developing an effective problem-solving model can be part of the performance task. The model can be used either to assess a student's problem-solving skills or to create a context for demonstrating their understanding of how to apply and evaluate specific concepts in various content areas.

Sample assessment tasks using Problem-solving Models

- Show your understanding of how to set goals by completing a problem-solving organizer outlining how you would save $100 for a school trip in June.
- Develop a plan for how you would stand up for yourself if a student in an older grade was threatening you after school. Use a visual organizer to show how you would solve this problem.
- Less than 20 percent of the citizens of your town voted in the last municipal election of your town. How could your local government encourage more people to participate in the next election?

Sample of completed Problem Solving Model

A. Describe the problem.

> *Need $100 for school trip by May 01.*

B. Potential solutions.

> - *Sell skateboard*
> - *Cash Canada Savings Bond*
> - *Earn $100 helping Bart deliver fliers ($25. for 4 months)*

C. Best solution

> *Earn money delivering fliers*

D. Action plan

> 1. *Talk to Bart.*
> 2. *Work 2 hrs. every Wed. (Jan. Feb. Mar. Apr.)*
> 3. *Put money in savings account*

E. Signs of success

> *Money in savings account*
>
> *Jan. 30 — $25* ☐   *Feb. 28 — $50* ☐   *March 30 — $75* ☐
> *April 30 — $100* ☐

See page 66 for the scoring rubric.

Solve the Problem

A. Describe the problem

B. Potential solutions

- _____
- _____
- _____

C. Best solution

D. Action plan

1. _____

2. _____

3. _____

E. Signs of success – how I will know if the problem is successfully solved

Scoring Rubric for a Problem-solving Organizer

4 (Standard of excellence)

- communicates careful and insightful analysis of problem to be solved
- identifies a range of interesting and feasible options
- identifies a best choice and convincingly communicates rationale for this choice
- develops a detailed and creative action plan
- identifies clear and convincing criteria to evaluate success of plan

3 (Exceeds acceptable standard)

- communicates careful analysis of problem to be solved
- identifies a range of feasible options
- identifies a best choice and communicates rationale for this choice
- develops a detailed action plan
- identifies clear criteria to evaluate success of plan

2 (Meets acceptable standard)

- identifies problem to be solved
- identifies more than one appropriate option
- identifies best choice
- develops a basic action plan
- identifies basic criteria to evaluate success of plan

1 (Needs improvement to meet acceptable standard)

- identifies problem to be solved
- identifies limited options that are inappropriate or vague
- identifies an inappropriate option as best choice
- action plan is vague, flawed, and/or lacks detail
- basic criteria to evaluate success of plan is vague, flawed and/or lacks detail

Map-your-point Organizers

☑ Knowledge   ☑ Comprehension   ☑ Application
☑ Analysis   ☑ Synthesis   ☑ Evaluation

Map-your-point organizers (see Teacher Tool #22, page 68) create frameworks for students to build positions and to organize evidence in support of their positions. Used as assessment tasks, these types of organizers create opportunities for students to demonstrate their ability to identify positions and logically and convincingly support their case without having to produce a formal written essay. For many students with weak writing skills, essay writing is neither a reliable nor an effective way to demonstrate their thinking and knowledge.

Sample assessment tasks using Map-your-point organizers

- Should pesticide use within city limits be banned? Use a visual organizer to support your position.
- Do you think you would have preferred life in Canada in the early 1900s or life in Canada today? Use a map-your-point organizer to explain which time period would be better for you and the reasons why.
- You have read the novel *Holes* in class and have watched the movie. Using examples from the novel and the movie decide which was better—the experience of reading the book or watching the movie—and fill in the chart to prove your point.

Sample of completed Map-your-point organizer

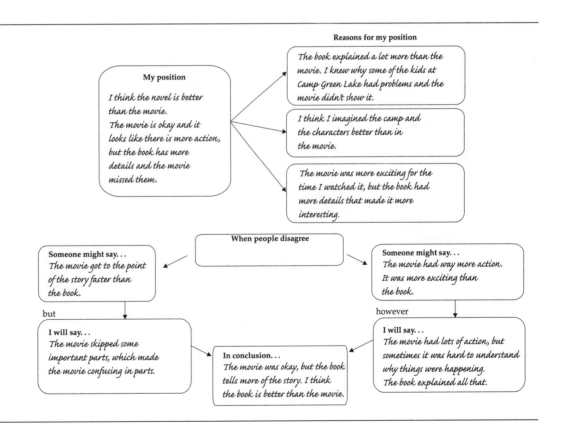

See page 69 for the scoring rubric.

Map Your Point

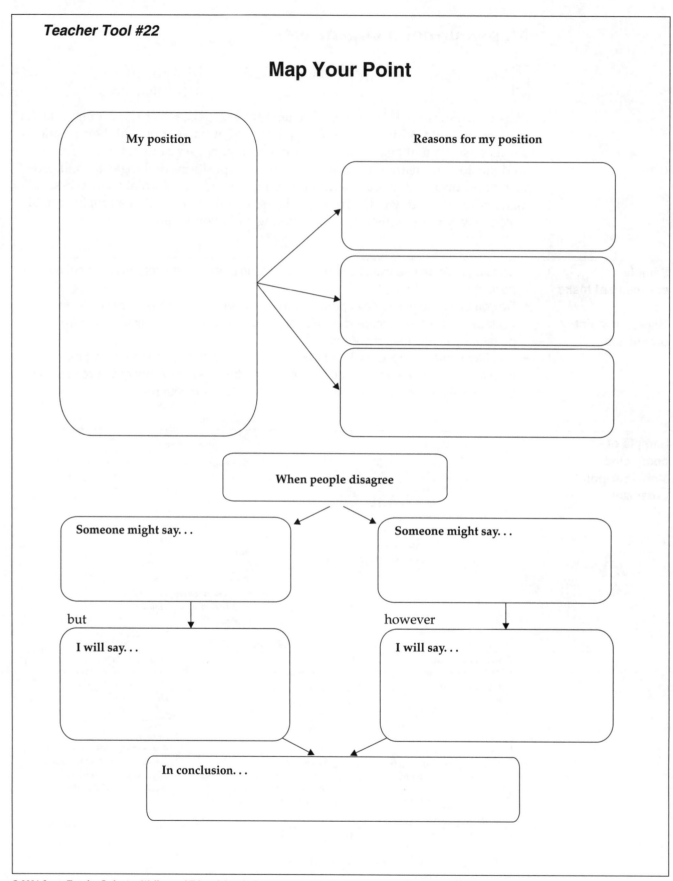

My position

Reasons for my position

When people disagree

Someone might say. . .

Someone might say. . .

but

however

I will say. . .

I will say. . .

In conclusion. . .

Scoring Rubric for a Map-your-point Organizer

4 (Standard of excellence)

- uses key words to plan and structure a convincing and logical argument
- opening position clearly states point of view and attracts reader's interest
- presents detailed facts or ideas to support point of view; uses examples and metaphors to communicate ideas clearly
- accurately and thoroughly identifies potential counter arguments
- offers convincing rebuttal to counter arguments
- conclusion is convincing combination of personal statement, prediction, and summary

3 (Exceeds acceptable standard)

- uses key words to plan and structure a logical argument
- opening position clearly states point of view
- presents detailed facts or ideas to support point of view; uses examples to support position
- accurately identifies counter arguments
- offers rebuttal to counter arguments
- conclusion is convincing and uses personal statement, prediction, or summary

2 (Meets acceptable standard)

- uses key words to plan and structure basic argument
- opening position states point of view
- presents facts or ideas to support point of view
- identifies counter arguments
- responds to counter arguments
- conclusion uses personal statement, prediction, or summary

1 (Needs improvement to meet acceptable standard)

- limited attempt to plan and structure basic argument
- opening position is unclear or confusing
- presents inaccurate or vague facts or ideas to support point of view
- limited attempt to identify counter arguments
- limited response to counter arguments
- conclusion is vague or confusing

T-charts

☑ Knowledge   ☑ Comprehension   ☑ Application
☑ Analysis   ☐ Synthesis   ☐ Evaluation

T-charts are tools to help students organize data. They can be used to describe what something looks and sounds like, or they can be used to compare and contrast different characters, situations, or issues. A simple T-chart (see Teacher Tool #24, page 71) has two columns with different headings, a triple T-chart (see Teacher Tool #25, page 72) has three columns with different headings.

Students can use T-charts to show their understanding of a particular topic or concept that cannot be summed up adequately in a few sentences. T-charts are especially useful for exploring abstract concepts that require reflection and descriptive analysis.

Sample assessment tasks using T-charts

- Show your understanding of what cooperation is by completing a T-chart of what cooperation looks like, sounds like and feels like, at school and in the community.
- Use a T-chart to show how one the main characters in the stories expresses his or her feelings. Record the name of the feeling in the first column, describe what the character says in the second column, what the character does in the third column and how other people react to these kinds of words and actions in the fourth column.
- Show your understanding of the research process by completing a T-chart with three headings:
  - questions I would ask
  - sources I could use
  - steps I would take to complete my project.

Sample of completed Triple T-chart

Triple T-Chart

Title/Topic: *COOPERATION*

Looks like:	Sounds like:	Feels like:
Kids smiling *Keeping hands and feet to yourself* *More than one person playing or working together*	*"It's your turn."* *"Let me help you."* *"What would you like to do?"*	*happy* *calm* *friendly*

See page 73 for the scoring rubric.

T-chart

Title/Topic: _____

Triple T-chart

Title/Topic:

Looks like:	Sounds like:	Feels like:

Scoring Rubric for a T-chart

4 (Standard of excellence)

- identifies multiple convincing and insightful examples of what a specific trait looks like/sounds like/feels like
- uses precise and detailed vocabulary to support description of examples

3 (Exceeds acceptable standard)

- identifies multiple convincing examples of what a specific trait looks like/sounds like/feels like
- uses detailed vocabulary to support description of examples

2 (Meets acceptable standard)

- identifies appropriate examples of what a specific trait looks like/sounds like/feels like
- uses appropriate vocabulary to support description of examples

1 (Needs improvement to meet acceptable standard)

- identifies examples of what a specific trait looks like/sounds like/feels like that are erroneous or inappropriate
- uses vocabulary that is vague and/or is incorrect

4

Building a Bank of Question Types

This chapter offers sample assessment tasks that can kick-start your thinking to create your own bank of types of questions. You can then use your question bank to build smart tests in any subject area across the grade levels.

The samples of types of questions are organized under the level of thinking the task demands. However, some of the 24 types of questions may be categorized under more than one level of thinking.

A fair assessment task is a familiar task, so be sure to use varied types and levels of question types throughout the school year. Students need lots of experience working with these different types of tasks independently, in partners and small groups, and as a guided class activity.

Knowledge

1. Defining Terms

Identify key terms that are essential for understanding a new unit of study. Design assessment tasks that give students a context and structure for demonstrating their knowledge and understanding of these terms.

Sample assessment task from a Grade 2 Math test	Draw a picture of each 3-D shape.		
	cone	sphere	cylinder

Sample assessment task from a Grade 6 Social Studies test	Show your understanding of the following election terms by using each word in an interesting and informative sentence. • ballot • platform • ward

2. Using Maps

Create a task to assess students' skills in using maps by adapting a classroom map activity; use an activity they may have done as a partner- or class-activity and ask students to complete it independently. Provide a clearly drawn map: either ask students to label sections or features of the map, or to have them use the map to find specific information.

Sample assessment tasks from a Grade 2 Social Studies test	A. Draw a red arrow on the globe to show the North Pole. B. Draw a green arrow on the globe to show the South Pole.	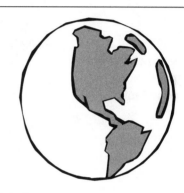

Sample assessment tasks from a Grade 6 Social Studies test	Find China on this map. What **continent** is it on? What **ocean** does it border? Which **hemisphere** is it in? Name two countries that are **neighbors** of China. Mark the approximate **location of where you** live with an X. How does China compare to Canada in its **proximity to** the equator? List two **coordinates** that would help you locate China on a map of the world. degrees longitude _____ latitude _____

3. Labeling a Diagram

Diagrams can create contexts for students to demonstrate their basic understanding of specific objects, systems, or processes.

Sample assessment task from a Grade 2 Science test

Label the body parts of the ant using the following words.

legs   abdomen   antennae   thorax   eye   head

Sample assessment task from a Grade 6 Science test

Label the four forces of flight on both the bird and the plane.

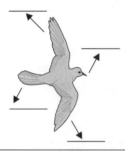
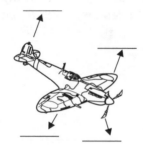

Comprehension

4. Sequencing Ideas

One way to demonstrate knowledge and understanding of a process is to put the separate elements of the process into the correct sequence. Many processes are not strictly linear and may be expressed with webs and diagrams using arrows and connecting words.

Sample assessment task from a Grade 2 Science test

Cut out the four pictures below and show how a **food chain** works by gluing the pictures in the correct order.

plant   snail   bird   sun

Sample assessment task from a Grade 4 Social Studies

Show at least four of the steps that might happen between the time a tree grows in the forest and the time it is a table in your house.

Tree in forest					Table in my house

Sample assessment task from a Grade 6 Science test

Write the names of living things that might be on each level of food web that has an owl at the top.

a) Consumer: owl ⟶ b) Secondary consumer: _____

c) Producer: _____

d) Decomposer: _____

5. Drawing Pictures

There are a number of concepts and processes that are difficult to explain in words alone and can be defined and explained more effectively with diagrams and pictures. Encourage students to label parts of a drawing that illustrate specific parts or aspects of a process or concept.

Sample assessment task from a Grade 2 Health test

Draw a picture of yourself and label at least two parts of your body where you feel stress the most.

Sample assessment task from a Grade 6 Science test

Make a drawing to show how people and trees depend on each other for the air they breath. Use the key words below to label the parts of your drawing.

carbon dioxide   oxygen   exhale   inhale

6. Identifying Examples

Generating lists of examples is a creative way to demonstrate understanding of specific concepts or skills. In order to this effectively, students need a clear context and a sample structure for organizing their information. It might also help to provide one or two samples of appropriate examples to demonstrate how specific or how detailed the examples need to be.

Sample assessment task from a Grade 4 Social Studies test

Complete the following chart by listing three examples of different services that communities organize to help families meet their needs. Give an example of how your family might use that service.

Service	How my family might use this service
City library	*take out books for science project*

Sample assessment task from a Grade 6 Science test

List the means of **propulsion** for the following things that fly:

flying squirrel   *the force of its jump as it pushes itself into the air*

jet   _____

_____

dirigible   _____

_____

paper airplane   _____

_____

helicopter   _____

_____

7. Filling in Missing Information

Challenge students to examine information and identify obvious patterns and/or sequences to answer the question "What is missing?" Use simple stories and incomplete diagrams, webs, or data graphs to create assessment tasks.

Sample assessment task from a Grade 3 Math test

What pattern do you see in the number pairs? Use the pattern to help you fill in the missing numbers. Choose your own numbers for the last two boxes, but make sure they fit the same pattern as the other number pairs.

7	11	14	10		25	
14	22	28		18		

Sample assessment task from a Grade 6 Science test

Celeste was tracking the phases of the moon during the month of October. Some nights were clear and she was able to record what she observed. Other nights were cloudy and she was unable to see the moon. She also fell asleep before she could do her recordings on three nights.

A. Help Celeste complete the drawings of the seven phases that she missed on the 4th, 16th, 19th, 20th, 21st, 23rd, and 28th days of the month.

B. The new moon was on the _____ day of the month.

C. The full moon was on the _____ day of the month.

Applying

8. Making Personal Connections

Create opportunities for students to transfer their learning from the classroom to their daily lives on the playground, at home, and in the community. Structure assessment tasks so that they create contexts for applying new knowledge to a variety of real-life situations.

Sample assessment tasks from a Grade 2 Science test

Describe three areas in your home where **insulation** is used.

Sample assessment tasks from a Grade 5 Social Studies test	A. Describe one idea or event that you found especially interesting in our unit on South America. Explain why. B. If you were visiting Brazil, what three things would you like to see and learn more about?

9. Applying Knowledge to Make a Change

Give students opportunities to apply knowledge in a variety of ways. Use assessment tasks that challenge them to demonstrate their understanding of a new concept by describing how it could be used to make a change. Create a context by identifying real-life examples of where these concepts might be applied.

Sample assessment tasks from a Grade 2 Science test	Describe three things you could do to make your classroom feel **cooler.** Describe three things you could do to make your living room feel **warmer.**

Sample assessment task from a Grade 6 Science test	Many athletes use the concept of **streamlining** to reduce drag to improve their performance. Choose one of the types of athletes from the list below and describe three **modifications** in behaviors or equipment that could improve that athlete's performance. cyclist skier bobsled driver sprinter speed skater swimmer

10. Using Other Sources of Information

Finding and using information from a variety of sources is a skill students need in order to apply and analyze information. Create assessment tasks by setting up situations for students to independently use familiar reference tools, such as charts, guides, or booklets, to gather and organize targeted information. Model effective organization of information by providing charts or tables for recording information. Include descriptive categories and appropriate recording space to cue students as to what information they need, how much they need to record, and what conclusions they need to draw.

Sample assessment task from a Grade 3 Health test	Use information from your healthy eating guide to plan one meal for your family. Draw the meal on a dinner plate and write three sentences explaining why you chose those foods.

Sample assessment task from a Grade 6 Science test	Use your tree booklet to find out the **similarities and differences** between poplar and birch trees. Organize your information on the chart below.

How they are different	
Poplar trees	Birch trees
1._____	1._____
2._____	2._____
3._____	3._____
How they are similar	
1._____	
2._____	
3._____	

11. Identifying Errors

Simple stories can be used to create assessment tasks that contain an error or puzzling situation for students to identify or solve by applying new knowledge and understanding.

Sample assessment task from a Grade 2 Science test	On her way to school Alison saw a tiny black creature on a green leaf. It had 2 body parts and 7 legs. What kind of animal do you think it was, and why might it have 7 legs?

Sample assessment task from a Grade 5 Math test	Simon checked out 57 library books last year. He wanted to know how many books would be checked out of the school library if all 682 students in the school read 57 books a year just like he did. When he did the math he came up with two different answers. Check his multiplication and circle any errors you find. Is either answer correct?

Answer A
$$\begin{array}{r} 682 \\ \times\,57 \\ \hline 4774 \\ 3310 \\ \hline 8094 \end{array}$$

Answer B
$$\begin{array}{r} 682 \\ \times\,57 \\ \hline 4774 \\ 3310 \\ \hline 8084 \end{array}$$

Analyzing

12. Comparing and Contrasting

Even very young children can look for similarities and differences. This task of breaking a concept into discrete parts and analyzing each part gives students opportunities to explore ideas in a deep and systematic way.

Sample assessment task from a Grade 2 Health test

On a chart, draw two ways you are similar to one person in your family and two ways you are different from that person.

How I'm **similar** to	How I'm **different** from

Sample assessment task from a Grade 4 Language Arts test

How are Snow White and Sleeping Beauty alike and how are they different? Complete a chart that compares and contrasts these two characters from our unit on Fairy Tales.

Snow White	Sleeping Beauty
How they are alike A. B. C.	
How they are different	
A.	A.
B.	B.
C.	C.

Sample assessment tasks from a Grade 6 Social Studies test

1. Describe three ways a typical Chinese family's home in the city would be different from a typical North American family's city home.
2. A cricket is popular pet in many Chinese homes. Why might this tiny insect be a more suitable pet than a typical Canadian kind of pet such as a cat or dog?
3. Like Canada, China has oil. However, China does NOT export much oil to other countries. Why?
4. Unlike Canada, China does NOT have a large forestry industry. Give two reasons why.

---

13. Identifying Attributes and Characteristics

Create assessment tasks that allow students to demonstrate their understanding of a concept by going beyond simply telling what something is to the more challenging task of identifying and/or describing the special characteristics of that concept.

Sample assessment task from a Grade 2 Science test	Small animals need homes that have A. _____ B. _____ C. _____ D. _____
Sample assessment tasks from a Grade 6 Social Studies	A. Describe three things that a candidate might do as part of his or her **election campaign.** B. Describe three personal or professional **qualities** that you think are important that an elected representative have.

14. Sorting and Classifying

Being able to sort and classify objects or concepts into specific categories demonstrates a basic understanding of separate elements and how they fit together to create a whole. Model systematic thinking by creating easy-to-use charts and tables for students to sort various types of information. Allow students to focus on the actual task of sorting by providing unambiguous and precise category headings. Ensure that the task is assessing the ability to sort (and students are not being rewarded or penalized for their ability to remember terms) by providing the information to be sorted in a separate box. When appropriate, add a supplemental task asking students to add one or two of their own examples to each of the categories.

Sample assessment task from a Grade 2 Health test	Sort the following snacks into one of the groups in your healthy eating guide. Add your own example of a food choice to each group.

apple   muffin   yogurt   banana   oatmeal cookie   beef jerky
orange juice rice   carrot   crackers   cheese   chocolate bar

Grain products	Vegetables and fruit	Milk products	Meat and alternatives	Other foods

Sample assessment task from a Grade 4 Spelling test

Sort the following spelling words on the chart below.

agree	reason	either	valley	genie
steal	season	teaching	beneath	neighbor

Add two of your own words under each of the headings.

Long e sounds		
e	ea	ee
ey	ie	e

Sample assessment task from a Grade 6 Science test

Show whether each body reflects or emits light by sorting each body into the correct column of the table below.

star	Polaris	asteroid	Mars
comet	Sun	Earth	meteor in Earth's atmosphere
meteor-in space	Moon		

Emits light	Reflects light

15. Demonstrating Attitudes

Many learning outcomes involve demonstrations of certain attitudes. One way to assess these types of outcomes is to create a context for demonstrating the attitude and then asking students to describe behaviors that would illustrate it.

Sample assessment task from a Grade 2 Health and Life Skills test

Use keywords and pictures to complete the following chart.

What children can do and say to create a safe and caring ...		
playground	classroom	home

| **Sample assessment task from a Grade 4 Physical Education test** | A. Give two examples of the types of encouraging words you can say to other players on your team. |

B. If I think the referee has made a wrong call, here are two smart things I can say to myself.

_____

_____

Synthesizing

16. Formulating Questions

Encourage higher-level thinking by challenging students to formulate questions to solve problems, find out more information, and/or demonstrate their knowledge of the depth and breadth of a specific topic or concept.

| **Sample assessment task from a Grade 2 Science test** | Miss Watson has a secret bug. Ask three questions that could help you find out what type of bug it is. The questions should be about the characteristics of the type of animals. (e.g., Does your bug have eight legs?) |

| **Sample assessment task from a Grade 5 Social Studies test** | In Grade 6 you will be researching and studying more about Kenya and other African countries. Think of five questions you would like to ask or ideas that would like to learn more about. |

17. What Might Happen If …?

Create opportunities for divergent thinking by designing assessment tasks that ask students to speculate on the interesting question, "What might happen if...?" Structure tasks so students have opportunities to make predictions and inferences based on their knowledge and understanding of new concepts.

Sample assessment task from a Grade 2 Science test	Describe what would happen if you left an ice cube on the table.
Sample assessment task from a Grade 4 Health test	What would happen if all the volunteers in your school decided to stop their work with students?
Sample assessment tasks from a Grade 6 Science test	Terra and Byron were hiking where there had been a forest fire two years before. They wondered what this part of the forest would be like in ten years.

1. Reforested areas can take
   A. five to 10 years to mature.
   B. 15 to 25 years to mature.
   C. 30 to 50 years to mature.
   D. 50 to 200 years to mature.

2. The young trees in this clearing would tend to stay the same shape over the next ten years because growth only occurs
   A. at the tips of the main stem and branches.
   B. at the tip of the main stem.
   C. at the tip of the branches.
   D. in the trunk.

3. In ten years there would NOT be a great deal more lichen than today because
   A. insects make homes in it.
   B. it grows so slowly.
   C. it prefers older trees.
   D. the deer would eat it.

4. If there was another fire in this part of the forest within the next ten years,
   A. the trees would all die out.
   B. there would no wildlife left.
   C. new bushes and shrubs might grow.
   D. the soil would wash away.

18. Identifying Advantages and Disadvantages

Identifying advantages and disadvantages requires a combination of thinking skills that includes divergent thinking, comparing and contrasting, decision-making, drawing conclusions, and making inferences. Design assessment tasks that create opportunities to use these skills by creating a clearly organized structure for students to use in organizing and recording their information.

Sample assessment tasks from a Grade 2 Science test	One good thing about having bees in the school playground is they can _____. One not-so-good thing about having bees in the school playground is they can _____.
Sample assessment task from a Grade 4 Social Studies test	Two reasons it would be fun or interesting to live in pioneer times are A. _____ B. _____ Two reasons it would be difficult to live in pioneer times are A. _____ B. _____
Sample assessment task from a Grade 6 Science test	List two advantages and two disadvantages of placing an instrument, such as the Hubbell telescope, in orbit around the Earth. <table><tr><td>Advantages</td><td>Disadvantages</td></tr><tr><td>1. _____</td><td>1. _____</td></tr><tr><td>2. _____</td><td>2. _____</td></tr></table>

19. Making Inferences

To make an inference is to "read between the lines" or use information and other evidence to draw a conclusion or come to a decision. Students need opportunities to push their understanding beyond the surface level and explore the "idea behind an idea."

Sample assessment task from a Grade 4 Health test	A new student has just arrived in your class and he doesn't speak very much English. Name five feelings this new student might have in this situation. (Include at least one positive feeling.) Describe one strategy you could use to help this student feel more welcome and comfortable.
Sample assessment task from a Grade 6 Social Studies test	From our study of ancient Greece, we know that many of our present-day ideas were influenced by the people of that era. Today, when we say someone has a **Spartan lifestyle** we mean _____.

20. Developing Action Plans

Higher levels of thinking involve putting new skills and concepts into action by developing a plan for solving a problem or making a change.

Sample assessment task from a Grade 2 Health test

Draw pictures and write words to show how you could solve the problem of a friend using your colored pencils without asking.

How I'll stay calm	What I'll say	What I'll try
	I feel _____ when _____ _____ I need _____ _____	

Sample assessment task from a Grade 5 Science test

You come into your classroom 8:42 a.m. and the contents of your desk are all over the floor. All other desks appear normal.

Using at least three steps for each action,
A. write down your plan for investigating this mystery.
B. explain why you would do each step of you action plan.
C. list the tools you need for each step.

What I would do	Why I would do this	Tools I would need
1. _____ _____ _____	_____ _____ _____	_____ _____ _____
2. _____ _____ _____	_____ _____ _____	_____ _____ _____
3. _____ _____ _____	_____ _____ _____	_____ _____ _____
4. _____ _____ _____	_____ _____ _____	_____ _____ _____

Evaluating

21. Interpreting Diagrams

Interpreting visual text is an increasingly important skill. Look for opportunities to build assessment tasks that challenge students to examine diagrams and other visual texts to extract information, make inferences, and draw conclusions. Ensure diagrams and drawings are clear and contain no distracting details that could mislead students. Structure tasks so students clearly understand what they are looking for and what they need to use the visual information for.

Sample assessment task from a Grade 2 Science test	Look at thermometer A. Circle the clothes that you would wear outside for that temperature. Look at thermometer B. Draw the kind of clothing you would wear outside for that temperature.

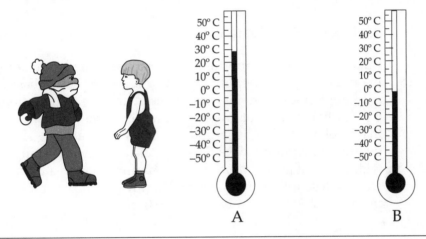

Sample assessment task from a Grade 6 Science test	Examine this picture of a tree cookie. List three things you can tell about the tree's age and growth pattern by looking at the tree cookie.

22. Applying Knowledge to Solve Problems

Create assessment tasks that challenge students to use new knowledge to solve problems. Create scenarios of situations that are personally relevant to students and can be realistically solved using students' current knowledge and skills.

Sample assessment task from a Grade 2 Health test

Use the word balloons to write three ways you can say no if another student asks you to do something at recess that is not safe.

Sample assessment task from a Grade 6 Social Studies test

I believe that after-school daycare programs are very important to the families of this city. I am concerned that our city council intends to cut funding to these programs by more than 20 percent over the next year. This is an important issue and I want to do something about it. Briefly describe three strategies I might use to influence government decision-making on this issue.

23. Interpreting Data Graphs

Data graphs create opportunities for students to identify, organize, and interpret information across the subject areas. Assessment tasks based on data graphs can encourage students to identify patterns, analyze information, and make inferences. Choose types of graphs that students are familiar with and include data that is relevant to students and what they are learning. These tasks can ask one question in different ways. They can also create interesting contexts by including a wide range of information that, if communicated in a traditional format such as a written description, might be too lengthy or complex for students to handle independently and within a limited time frame.

Sample assessment task from a Grade 3 Math test

Our class is having a pizza party. We asked students about their favorite pizza and recorded their answers on this chart. Use this chart to answer questions 1 and 2.

Type of pizza	
Ham and cheese	☺☺☺☺☺☺☺☺
Salami	☺☺☺☺☺
Mushroom	☺☺☺☺
Tomato and red pepper	
Do NOT like pizza	☺☺

☺ means one person

1. What kind of pizza did the MOST people choose as their favorite? _____
2. How many people choose the salami pizza? _____

This graph shows the length of the shadows cast by a stick at various times throughout the day.

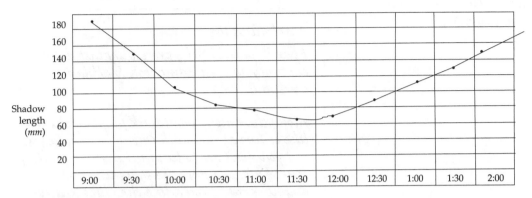

A. Describe the **pattern** that the data shows.
B. Using the information from this graph, what can you **infer** about the weather on the day the data was collected?
C. This data was collected in the early summer. What would be **different** if the data was collected in mid winter?

24. Exploring Issues

Students in Grades 4, 5, and 6 are ready to begin using new knowledge and skills to explore social issues. Before they are able to do this independently, they will need lots of classroom experience identifying and discussing issues in a mediated situation. Exploring issues means being able to see more than one side of a particular point-of-view, so assessment tasks should provide opportunities for students to show their understanding of more than one perspective. Choose issues that match the interests and concerns of the students' age group and are within the scope of their personal experience. Provide a structure for the response that clearly identifies what and how many points they must address.

A. Should children 12 years and older be allowed to vote? Give two reasons for each side of the argument.

Reasons why children over 12 should be allowed to vote		Reasons why children over 12 should NOT be allowed to vote	
1.	❏ fact ❏ opinion	1.	❏ fact ❏ opinion
2.	❏ fact ❏ opinion	2.	❏ fact ❏ opinion

B. Check the correct box to show whether each of your reasons is a fact or opinion.

Read the following letter to the editor published in the *Edmonton Journal*, November 27, 1997.

> **A dolphin's life**
>
> I participated in the protest against dolphin captivity at West Edmonton Mall last weekend.
>
> Along the route I would ask people if they'd like to live at the mall. One woman said yes. But you don't get to live in the entire mall, of course, just one store the same size as the dolphin's tank. You'd like that life? Really? I find that absolutely amazing.
>
> Lynn Devline

A. What is the main issue that this letter is discussing? _____

B. Briefly describe the two sides of the issues.

First point of view (the opinion of the letter writer)	Alternative point of view (the opinion of people who not agree with the letter writer)

C. In your opinion, should a bylaw be passed to resolve this issue? Explain why or why not.

_____

_____

_____

D. If you were a city councillor, what might you do about this issue?

_____

_____

5

Setting the Stage for Success

Success builds on success. If students have done poorly on tests in the past, it's unreasonable to expect them to suddenly start doing well. And when we lower our expectations for students, they tend to do just what is expected of them. Past failures, combined with low expectations from teachers, parents, and students themselves, hinder learning and test performance.

An essential component for creating and maintaining high expectations for students is a positive and supportive learning environment. There are a number of practical strategies for everyday classroom work that can create support, raise expectations, and set the stage for successful learning and test performance. These strategies include

- making good questions a regular part of classroom learning
- helping students organize information
- helping students learn about learning
- thoughtful scheduling of tests
- in-class reviews

Using Good Questions

Asking good questions is a key component of developing smart tests. To encourage active learning, you need to ask thought-provoking, open-ended questions as part of your instructional practice. It is also important that students have opportunities to develop their questioning skills. Students need to learn how to ask questions that help them better understand content and begin to make clear connections between diverse thoughts.

You need to be aware of various types of questions so you can form questions appropriate to the context and content of skills and concepts under study, and can match the abilities and interests of the students. By varying the questions you ask, you can elicit a wide range of responses. This creates opportunities for students to develop a broader range of thinking, reasoning, and problem-solving skills.

Students Answering Questions

All students need opportunities to participate in class discussion and contribute ideas and thoughts by answering questions. To fully participate, some students will need more encouragement and support. Involving everyone in the answering of questions keeps all students more accountable for thinking about and answering questions; it ensures more active engagement of all students. Develop classroom routines and rituals that ensure all students feel comfortable and confident answering questions.

- Consider using name cards that you shuffle and draw to make sure you are asking questions of all students, not just the few who are always eager to answer questions and are skilled at getting the attention of teachers.
- Explicitly teach students effective listening behaviors, such as looking at the speaker, keeping hands and feet quiet, asking questions in their heads, and waiting their turn.
- Use routines, such as round robins, that let students know they each will have an opportunity to answer a question.
- Keep the questions as open-ended as possible. This ensures there are fewer wrong answers, and open-ended questions tend to generate more divergent thinking and discussion.

When You Ask Questions

- Critical and creative thinking and reflection take time: when asking a question, a good rule of thumb is to wait at least three seconds (or as long as ten seconds) to ensure that all students have the chance to think about the question.
- Encourage students to "think in their heads" and discourage random call-outs from individual students. Let students know how you will be soliciting answers—you may invite students who have their hands raised to share their answers or you may decide to draw cards or do a round robin.
- Get as many and as varied answers to questions as possible. Encourage students to build upon one another's responses.

Students need to learn that there is usually a range of possible and acceptable answers, although some answers are better than others. They also need to understand that answers can change over time, in different situations, and with different information.

Students Asking Questions

Encourage students to ask questions—both of you and of one another. Students derive meaning and knowledge by asking questions and they must learn to ask good questions if they are to become independent thinkers and learners. The ability to recognize problems and form questions is key to developing problem-solving and critical-thinking skills. Constructing effective questions and using them to find possible answers is a powerful strategy that helps students connect, interpret, and apply new information in new situations.

Give explicit instruction in questioning by introducing students to the range of possible question types, based on Bloom's taxonomy (page 17). Younger children can learn to ask questions that require thinking, not just a "yes" or "no" response. Students need opportunities to develop their questioning skills by

- identifying a problem
- formulating a key question to explore the problem
- collecting all the necessary information
- arriving at an acceptable answer to the questions
- understanding that at another time they may work with the questions again and that, because of new information or a different situation, they may come up with different or additional answers to the same questions

Encourage students to ask questions about everything and anything by establishing that all questions are worthwhile. Model a willingness to explore questions by admitting when you do not know something. Situations in which you don't have the answer at the tip of your fingers are opportunities to model how to actively explore a question and look for possible answers.

Teacher Tool #27, on page 97, will help you assess how you are using questions in your teaching practice.

Helping Students Organize Information

Students need organized information if they are to effectively prepare for assessment tasks. Help students set up notebooks that are easy to keep organized. Consider using a color-coding system, such as green notebooks for Science and orange for Math. Help students set up a table of contents for each notebook, and encourage them to title and date all written assignments and class work. Part of an in-class review for a unit test can include putting notebooks in order, ensuring all assignments are complete, and making sure individual students have copies of all handouts and class notes.

Organized notebooks are helpful as part of in-class reviews because they allow students to quickly locate and review material. They provide accurate and complete information for students to take home as part of their study plan. As each unit of study is completed, students can remove the related material from their notebooks, clip it together, and store it in a clearly marked file folder for future reference and review.

Students in Grades 4 to 6 need to learn a variety of strategies for taking notes from class discussion, assigned reading, and learning activities. Student-made notes can be valuable study tools.

Tables of Contents

A table of contents for the primary grades might be a simple numbered list of assignments completed as part of the unit study.

Sample table of contents for a Grade 2 Science unit

Name _____   Date _____

Science Topic: Hot and Cold Temperature

Table of Contents

1. Measuring Temperature
2. one Ptato two Ptato
3. Around the school
4. Hot House / cold House
5. Body Temperature
6. Safety

_____
_____
_____

For students in Grades 4 to 6 a table of contents might include completed assignments, in-class notes, handouts, project work, and study plans. See the sample below for a table of contents for a Grade 6 Science unit on air, aerodynamics, and flight.

Sample table of contents for Grade 6 Science unit

Air, Aerodynamics and Flight

Table of contents	Complete
1. Amazing Air	☐
2. Flight (what I want to know)	☐
3. Up and away	☐
4. Outline	☐
5. Poster information	☐
6. Air (Bernouilli's principle)	☐
7. Getting down safely	☐
8. Balloon Adventures (mind map)	☐
9. How things fly (notes from presentations)	☐
10. Helicopter Challenge	☐
11. Concorde instructions (and model)	☐
12. Unit review	☐
13. Study plan.	☐
14. Using your Amazing Air knowledge	☐
15. Straw flyer investigations	☐
16. Presentation notes (+4)	☐
	☐

How Am I Using Questioning in My Teaching?

1. Is the classroom learning environment safe and supportive, and does it encourage all students to ask and explore the questions they want and need to?   ❏ yes   ❏ not yet

2. Are my questions clear, and my vocabulary and examples appropriate for the interests and abilities of this group of students?   ❏ yes   ❏ not yet

3. Are students getting enough factual information to have a solid foundation for asking questions and discussing new skills and concepts?   ❏ yes   ❏ not yet

4. Is there equal opportunity for all students to answer questions and participate in discussion?   ❏ yes   ❏ not yet

5. Do I wait three to ten seconds after asking questions so that all students have an opportunity to think about the questions?   ❏ yes   ❏ not yet

6. Is there ample opportunity for students to discuss and explore their ideas with classmates and with me?   ❏ yes   ❏ not yet

7. Do I show students that I don't have all the answers, and do I model different ways to find answers to questions?   ❏ yes   ❏ not yet

8. Do students have opportunities to learn about particular questioning strategies?   ❏ yes   ❏ not yet

Helping Students Learn about Learning

Students are most likely to perform well on assessment tasks when they are doing their best in classroom learning activities all day, everyday, all school year. Maintaining this kind of momentum requires a great deal of effort and motivation. Students need continual opportunities to

- assess their own work
- ask for feedback
- reward themselves for completing work and doing a good job
- work within time limits
- keep working when they feel stuck
- let go of their mistakes
- take learning risks
- learn about learning

Look for authentic opportunities throughout the school day to introduce practical strategies that will enhance students' personal capacity for learning and help them develop strong work habits and positive attitudes. Make these strategies part of classroom routine and rituals. For example, when an individual student feels stuck, they can try one or more steps from Student Tool #2: What to Do when You're Stuck (page 99). Teachers can reinforce these types of strategies by providing explicit instruction and guided practice, displaying posters outlining the strategies in the classroom, and cueing students to use the strategies at appropriate times throughout the instructional day.

Scheduling Tests

How tests are scheduled can affect student success. To help young students build strong review and study skills, do an in-class review at the beginning of the week, and make study and review part of the regular homework program for the three to four days preceding the test. Coordinate the assessment schedule so students are preparing for one test at a time and are writing only one test per day.

To help students and their families develop effective study routines, schedule major tests toward the end of the week rather than for Mondays. Weekends are often busy times for families, and Saturdays and Sundays tend to be less structured than weekdays. Families often find it easier to maintain a regular study schedule on weekdays.

If possible, schedule major tests during the first part of the school day.

Doing In-class Reviews

How familiar and comfortable students are with new information obviously affects how well students do on a test. In-class reviews are an essential part of smart tests, and contribute to student success. Structured reviews create

What to Do when You're Stuck

1. Read the directions **two** more times.

2. Highlight key words.

3. Look at an example and talk the steps through in your mind.

4. Copy the sample question and work it through on your own.

5. Give yourself a fresh start. Copy the question or try writing your answer on another piece of paper, and then work it through by yourself.

6. Mark the question with a star (*), go to the next question, and come back to the missed question later.

opportunities for students to revisit skills and concepts, and they expand and reinforce student understanding of new ideas and information. Most importantly,
reviews focus students' attention on key concepts and skills, creating a tool that
students can share with their parents as they review the material at home. A good
review will provide parents with a blueprint of specific skills and concepts they
can actively discuss, review, and rehearse with their children.

See Chapter 6 for organizing in-class reviews and using test preparation as part
of the homework program.

6

Helping Students Prepare for Tests

The three key qualities that affect test-taking success are desire, preparation, and confidence. Discuss each of these qualities with students.

- **Desire** is wanting to do well and believing that doing well on a test matters.
- **Preparation** is engaging in classroom discussion, learning activities, and assignments before the test. Preparation is also the study and review students do before the test, and how they get ready for the test, including getting a good night's sleep and eating a healthy breakfast.
- **Confidence** is the belief that individual effort can make a difference, and that success is possible.

Work together as a class to generate a T-chart of what each of these three qualities looks like, sounds like, and feels like in relation to active learning and successful test performance.

Sample of completed T-chart on Participation	Participation	
	Looks like	Sounds like
	– eyes on the speaker to listen – raising hand to answer questions and share ideas – finishing assignments – writing test date on calendar – taking folder home to study	"I'm ready to work!" "I have an idea . . ." "I finished this activity." "What do I need to know for my test?"

"There is no better way to master a subject than to ask and debate fundamental questions about what is most important about that subject—and how someone could tell if they had mastered it." (Brown, 1989) Encourage students to get ready for a test by asking themselves "What do I need to know?" and "How can I show what I know?"

Students who are involved in the creation of some of their own assessment tasks can reflect on what they have learned and make judgments about it. As a class, brainstorm potential assessment tasks and sample test questions that show that students understand and can use the new skills, information, and concepts they have been learning in class. This can be as simple as brainstorming sample questions, or as complex as developing step-by-step assessment tasks that teachers can adapt and format as unit tests.

In-class Reviews

Students need to revisit and review new information and ideas so they can demonstrate their knowledge and understanding. Doing in-class reviews for major tests ensures that all students are focused on the specific skills and concepts that will be assessed. It also creates an outline that they can take home and use as a study tool.

In-class review gives you opportunities to check for understanding and, if necessary, reteach, reinforce, or reframe any material that students are still unsure of. Reviews also provide an authentic context for students to learn about different kinds of assessment tasks and try them out. Students should have experience using tasks before they are expected to do them independently in testing situations.

Reviewing with Younger Students

Younger students need guided reviews that closely parallel the assessment tasks they are preparing for. By completing these reviews as a class, students can discuss how to approach different types of questions, where to look for different types of information, and what is important to record as an answer.

Prepare a review worksheet and provide students with copies. Display the review on an overhead and work through the questions as a class, discussing and recording possible answers for each item.

Encourage students to actively participate in the review by

- identifying where the needed information might be (in a completed assignment, on a chart paper in the classroom, in the textbook)
- sharing answers
- drawing diagrams or webs on an overhead transparency so all students can see it.

Some students will enjoy the challenge of working ahead on questions and then coming back to check their answers against the review completed by the rest of the class. It's important that students have accurate and complete information to take home for their review.

Emphasize that there is often more than one correct answer to a question, and that individual students can use different words, and sometimes different ideas, to show their knowledge and understanding.

The sample that follows is an in-class review for a Grade 2 Social Studies test on communities. The teacher used class discussion to generate sample answers for each part of the review and recorded this information on an overhead transparency. Each student had a copy of the review, chose sample answers from the teacher's modeling, and recorded this on the copy they took home for review.

Sample in-class review for a Grade 2 Social Studies test

Social Studies Review
Communities Nearby

Our unit test is on _____. (date)
We recommend that you review _____ minutes per night for _____ nights.
(This review replaces home reading and spelling words for the week.)

You need
❑ Social Studies notebook
❑ *Communities in Our World* textbook

Here is what you need to be able to do:
A. Write the name of your community
B. Write or sing your favorite two lines of the national anthem and draw a picture to show what the words mean to you.
C. Write your complete address.
D. Use key words and drawings to describe the two communities we studied:
   • What the land is like
   • Kind of jobs people have
   • What people do for fun
   • How people learn
   • Two ways the communities are similar to one another
   • Two ways the communities are different
E. Show where the North and South Pole are on this picture of a globe.

Label the four directions on this compass.

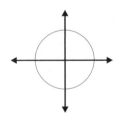

We have also been practising the following skills in class and you will get to use them on your test:
• Look at a picture of a community and tell what you can learn from the picture.
• Look at a picture map of a community and tell what you can learn from the map.
• Record information on a chart.

Parent signature _____

Reviewing with Older Students

Students in Grades 4 to 6 are able to actively participate in identifying key concepts and skills for the review. These students can also learn to develop and use a study organizer for major tests. They will need instruction and guidance the first few times, but eventually they will be able to complete most of the information working on their own or with a partner.

Provide students with a copy of Student Tool #3: Study Organizer (page 105) to record an outline of the content they are expected to know on the test. Use class notes, textbooks, and discussion to work together as a class, outlining all the key concepts that have been covered in the unit. Encourage students to record keywords rather than complete answers. Keywords will act as memory triggers and will encourage students to think about the answers, rather than try to memorize a specific answer.

Begin the review by having students brainstorm a list of all the specialized terms from the unit. Next, have them go through their notebooks and text and identify concepts that can be compared and contrasted. Talk about the "big ideas" in the unit and list the concepts that students might be asked to explain or describe on a test. Depending on the subject area, students can also identify concepts they might have to draw and label, or concepts and skills they might have to demonstrate.

Students can take the study organizer home and use it to talk through new information and make up questions to ask themselves.

Sample study organizer for a Grade 6 Science test

Student Tool #3

Study Organizer

Topic _____ *TREES & FORESTS* _____

My test will be on _____ *Monday, November 13* _____

To review for this test I should refer to _____ *my folder* _____

A. DEFINITIONS/TERMS	(Know what these words
• *habitat*	*mean and be able to use*
• *photosynthesis*	*them.*)
• *nutrient cycle* • *food web*	
• *producer / consumer / decomposer*	

B. CLASSIFY	(Be able to compare and con-
• *deciduous or coniferous*	*trast – know the similarities*
• *producer or consumer or decomposer*	*and differences.*)
• *identify leaves* *shapes arrangements*	

C. EXPLAIN	("What if . . ." "Tell why . . ."
• *what tree rings (cookies) tell about growth*	"Give reasons . . .")
• *how plants make food*	

D. DRAW (and label)	DEMONSTRATE
• *food web*	• *use keys to*
• *oxygen exchange*	*identify trees*

Student Tool #3

Study Organizer

Name: _____   Date: _____

Topic _____

My test will be on _____

To review for this test I should refer to _____

A. DEFINITIONS/TERMS	*(Know what these words mean and be able to use them.)*

B. CLASSIFY	*(Be able to compare and contrast – know the similarities and differences.)*

C. EXPLAIN	*("What if . . ." "Tell why . . ." "Give reasons . . .")*

D. DRAW *(and label)*	DEMONSTRATE

Take-home Review

Another approach to test review is to develop a study organizer that can be assigned as homework for the three to four nights leading up to a test. A take-home review could involve generating questions or completing assessment tasks, such as answering questions, creating webs, or making lists. If possible, make time available in class each day for students to share the information they have compiled the night before—as a class, in small groups, or with a partner. Creating opportunities to hear and see how others approach and interpret specific kinds of information and questions can be a valuable learning experience for students.

The first sample that follows shows a how a Grade 5 group of students organized their review of a unit on Canadian geography by generating ten new questions each night. The second sample (on pages 107–108) shows how a group of Grade 6 students did short assignments each night to prepare for a unit test on ancient Greece.

Sample take-home review for a Grade 5 Social Studies test

Social Studies Review

Topic: Canada and its geography

My test is on _____. (date)

Use your notes and textbook to find information to develop **thinking questions**. You don't have to write down the answers for each question, but you will have to find the information and think about it to make sure your question makes sense. Bring your questions to class the next day so you can share them with your classmates.

This is not a memory test—it is a test to show how well you can find and use information. During the test you will be able to use an atlas to help you find information.

Tuesday

Write ten questions that explore how geography can affect people's lives. For example:

- *If you wanted to be a farmer, what region of Canada might you choose to live in? Explain why.*
- *What areas of Canada would mountain climbers most like to visit?*
- *Why is it often more expensive to build houses in Canada's North than in most other regions of the country?*

Wednesday

Write ten questions comparing and/or contrasting two or more regions. For example:

- *Describe three ways the geography of the Pacific coast is similar to the Atlantic coast, and three ways it is different.*
- *What geographic features do each of the Atlantic provinces share?*
- *Compare the geography of three major cities in Canada.*

Thursday

Take home the Canadian Atlas. Write ten questions that could be answered by looking at one or more of the maps of Canada that are in the atlas. For example:

- *If you lived in Winnipeg, what would be the three closest cities?*
- *What areas of Canada have natural gas reserves?*
- *Find the longest river in Canada and list all the regions it travels through.*

Sample take-home review for a Grade 6 Social Studies test

Social Studies Review

Ancient Athens

My unit test is on _____. (date)

My goal is to score _____ % on my unit test.

Use this outline to help you review for your test.

	Topic	Time spent	Student and parent initials
Monday	how the climate and land affected life		
Tuesday	Olympic games		
Wednesday	slavery, life in Athens		
Thursday	government, influences today		

The questions on your unit test might include

- sorting charts
- lists
- true and false
- definitions
- short answers
- multiple choice
- compare and contrast charts

If you can think about and talk about the information in this booklet, you will have all the information you need to correctly answer all the test questions and show your understanding of how people in ancient Athens lived.

Your Social Studies notebook is an important study tool!

	Yes	Not yet
• I have all assignments in my notebook. (Check Table of Contents and circle any missing items.)	❏	❏
• All of my assignments are completed to the best of my ability.	❏	❏

Monday
- Use a web to describe the **climate** and **geography** of Greece.
- Make smaller webs to show how the climate and geography of ancient Athens affected **travel**, **buildings**, **farming,** and **trading**.
- Describe three additional aspects of life that climate and geography affected.

Tuesday
- Why were the **Olympic games** important to the people of ancient Athens?
- Use a Venn diagram or other organizer to show how these ancient games are similar to and different from today's Olympics.

Wednesday
- Make up five thinking questions about **slavery** in ancient Athens.
- Use a Venn diagram to compare and contrast **daily life in Athens** 200 BC and **Sparta** 200 BC

Thursday
- Use the Democracy in Ancient Greece web we made in class to explain how the **government in ancient Athens** worked to another person in your family.
- Describe five ways the ancient Greeks have influenced our life today.

Special terms in this unit—can you explain each one?

- assembly
- democracy
- helots
- city-state
- philosophy
- AD
- myths and legends

Add other words to this list.

When students are actively involved in the development of a study review (versus receiving a prepared review from the teacher) they are more likely to understand

- the scope and depth of the material they will need to review
- where to look for information
- how to accurately predict the type of assessment tasks they will be asked to do.

Study Skills

An in-class review provides a *tool* for studying, but students also need a *process* for studying. They need explicit instruction in specific strategies they can use to review information for tests. Strategies need to tap into different learning styles and create opportunities for actively engaging students, enhancing understanding, applying new skills and concepts, and helping students remember what they are learning and studying.

Introduce various study strategies throughout the school year and give students opportunities to practise these strategies. Make reflection and review part of your regular classroom practice, so students gain confidence in using these study strategies and can use them independently at home.

Develop a handout of favorite study strategies that students can take home to review with their parents. See Home Tool #1: Ten Smart Study Tips on page 109. Students need to learn a number of strategies to review material. Introduce and practise these study tricks in class, so students can begin using them at home independently.

Highlighting and Webbing

Highlighting key words creates opportunities for students to review new information. They can then use highlighted key words to create webs. By reorganizing the information and putting it into their own words, students are making the ideas easier to understand and remember.

Use an easy and interesting piece of text to teach students how to highlight key words. If students cannot highlight directly on text, make a photocopy of the page

Ten Smart Study Tricks

1. Highlight key words: Read over notes. Highlight key words.

2. Web ideas: Make a web for individual topics.

3. Make flash cards: Make up flash cards for special words and drawings.

4. Ask questions: Make up questions for each topic. Ask each of the questions at least three different ways.

5. Play Jeopardy: Use key words as answers and make up a question for each.

6. Review worksheets: Review all worksheets and written assignments in the unit. Cover up the answers and try them again. Change one activity on the worksheet and complete it.

7. Make clozes: Make up fill-in-the-blank statements.

8. Practise drawings: Practise drawing any diagrams from the unit. Label all the parts and explain the diagram.

9. Create practice tests: Make up a practice test.

10. Be a teacher: Teach someone else the information.

for each of them. Or use an overhead transparency sheet: place the clear sheet over the text and use an overhead marker to highlight key words. When students are finished with the transparencies, they can be washed off and reused.

Sample of highlighting to prepare for a Grade 4 Science test

Simple Machines

A simple machine is any device that helps us to perform our work more easily when effort or force is applied to it to move a load. A screw, wheelbarrow, a bottle opener and gears are all simple machines. To make any of these simple machines do work for us, we need to apply effort or energy to it. This effort or energy is called a *force*. These simple machines allow us to use a smaller force to move a larger load. They can help us change the direction of the force to move a load and they can help us move loads faster. Simple machines are very helpful.

To help students learn how to highlight and web simple information on a topic they are studying, give step-by-step instructions:

1. Quickly read the paragraph or section of text (this is called skimming.)
2. Identify the key idea; you will use this as a title for your web.
3. Find the key words in each sentence. Aim for one to five words per sentence.
4. Ask yourself, "Do each of these words provide an important piece of information about the main topic?"
5. Highlight these words with your highlighter pen.
6. Use your highlighter pen sparingly. You only want to highlight key words—not whole phrases or sentences. Here is an example.
7. Start with your title and organize the highlighted words into a web or list.

Sample web to prepare for a Grade 4 Science test

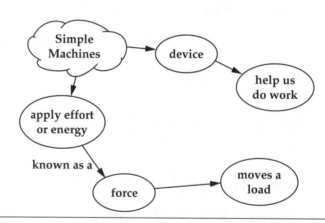

Encourage students to share completed webs with one another. Have them discuss how webs will differ according to student and information. Debate the strengths and limitations of different formats so students can make the best choices of types of webs or organizers to match both their individual learning needs and the specific types of information or task.

Highlighting key words and webbing can also be an effective strategy for gathering and organizing research information, developing speaking notes for a presentation, or writing a story or essay. The combination of the tasks enhances both understanding and memory of new information, because it encourages students to interact with information and ideas at least three different ways, including reading, rereading, writing, organizing in a web, and sharing information with others.

Study Plans

Help students create study plans like Student Tool #4: My Study Plan (page 112) so they can track how they used their review time. Encourage students to study for frequent short periods rather than one long session. Younger students need sessions of only 15 to 20 minutes; older students may be able to actively review for up to one hour. Build an element of accountability into the study plan by creating columns for student and parent signatures.

Test-taking Strategies

Students will need instruction in general test-taking strategies. There is an abundance of research available on what successful students do during tests. Do your own research on effective strategies for writing tests and choose the ones that best fit your students' needs. Review these tips with students before each major test. As students become more familiar with these test-taking strategies they can become involved: making posters for classroom display, developing student tip sheets, or taking turns leading the review of tips with either the whole class or in small groups.

General strategies that are most helpful to elementary students focus on attention to detail, stick-to-itness, and maintaining a positive attitude. Use Student Tool #5: Tips on Test Taking (page 113) to share strategies with students.

SCORER

Teach the SCORER strategy outlined in Home Tool #2 (page 114), so students have an acronym to remind themselves what to do during a test.

Checking Work

Teach the meaning of "check your work." Model how to review completed questions. Encourage students to quickly read over each answer again, testing it against the question. They can ask themselves questions such as the following:

- "Is this the answer I meant to mark?"
- "Does this sound right?"
- "Could I think about the question in another way?"
- "Do I need to add more information?"
- "Are all my questions filled in?"

Use Student Tool #6: Are You Using your Test Smarts? (page 115) to help students identify what they need to be doing as they review their test.

My Study Plan

Name: _____   Date: _____

	What study tricks did you use?	How long did you review?	Student signature	Parent initials
Monday				
Tuesday				
Wednesday				
Thursday				

Date of test _____

Unit/topic _____

Materials I will need to review _____

Ten Smart Study Tricks

1. **Highlight key words**: Read over notes. Highlight key words.

2. **Web ideas:** Make a web for individual topics.

3. **Make flash cards**: Make up flash cards for special words and drawings.

4. **Ask questions**: Make up questions for each topic. Ask each of the questions at least three different ways.

5. **Play Jeopardy**: Use key words as answers and make up a question for each.

6. **Review worksheets:** Review all worksheets and written assignments in the unit. Cover up the answers and try them again. Change one activity on the worksheet and complete it.

7. **Make clozes:** Make up fill-in-the-blank statements.

8. **Practise drawings:** Practise drawing any diagrams from the unit. Label all the parts and explain the diagram.

9. **Create practice tests:** Make up a practice test.

10. **Be a teacher:** Teach someone else the information.

Tips on Test Taking

- Read all directions TWICE.

- Highlight key words.

- Pay special attention to words in **bold**, *italics*, or CAPITALS.

- Read and review all the important clues in charts, pictures, graphs, and maps.

- When there is one piece of information that will be used to answer more than one question, reread the information as you work through each of the questions.

- If there is a word that you can't read or don't understand, read all the other words around it and ask yourself, "What word would make the most sense here?'

- Mark any question you find difficult, skip it, and come back to it at the end of the test.

- Some test questions have more than one step and ask you to consider a number of pieces of information. On scrap paper, jot down notes for each step of the question. Use this information to find your answer.

- Talk through your plan in your head. For example:

    "First I have to find out _____, then take that number and _____..."

    "To find out _____ I need to _____."

- If you are unsure of the question make a smart guess. Do not leave any questions unanswered.

- Keep working. If you finish early, reread each question and answer to make sure you have the complete answer.

SCORER

S = Schedule your time.

Look over the whole test. Decide how much time you have for each question. Use all the time given.

C = Clue words give you help.

Sometimes a word in the question will help you think of the answer.

O = Omit difficult questions.

Stay calm. Mark questions you don't know with a star (*). Keep going and then come back to skipped questions when you are finished the other questions.

R = Read directions carefully.

Highlight or circle key words in the directions. Visualize the steps in your mind.

E = Estimate your answers.

Read a difficult question through three times. If you don't know the answer, make a best guess and ask yourself, "Does this make sense?"

Check the value of the question. If it is worth three points make sure you have three points in your answer.

Try not to leave any blanks or unanswered questions.

R = Review your work.

Read over your answers three times. Ask, "Is this what I want to say? Does it make sense? Am I missing any information? Will someone else be able to read and understand my answers?"

Are You Using your Test Smarts?

Name: _____   Date:_____

A. Before the test:

1. Did I review two to three nights before the test?   ❏ yes   ❏ no

2. Did I ask my parents for help reviewing for the test?   ❏ yes   ❏ no

3. Did I take home my review and other information I would
   need for reviewing?   ❏ yes   ❏ no

4. Did I have a good sleep the night before?   ❏ yes   ❏ no

5. Did I have a healthy breakfast this morning?   ❏ yes   ❏ no

6. Did I bring to school all the materials I would need?   ❏ yes   ❏ no

7. Did I think positive thoughts to myself?   ❏ yes   ❏ no

B. During the test:

1. Did I read and follow the directions carefully?   ❏ yes   ❏ no

2. Did I use positive self-talk to encourage myself?   ❏ yes   ❏ no

3. Did I use my time well?   ❏ yes   ❏ no

4. Did I complete the test on time?   ❏ yes   ❏ no

5. Did I give each question my best try?   ❏ yes   ❏ no

6. Did I concentrate on the test and keep my focus?   ❏ yes   ❏ no

7. Did I understand the directions?   ❏ yes   ❏ no

8. Did I understand the questions on the test?   ❏ yes   ❏ no

9. Did I have enough time to finish?   ❏ yes   ❏ no

10. Did I carefully check my work by reading over each question
    answer a second time?   ❏ yes   ❏ no

Types of Assessment

Students need explicit instruction in how to approach specific types of assessment tasks. This information may need to be revisited several times throughout the school year, particularly if certain types of assessment tasks are not used in the classroom on a regular basis. There are a number of helpful tips and strategies that students can learn about multiple-choice tasks, true/false tasks, and essay or long-answer tasks.

Multiple-choice Tasks

A multiple-choice task consists of two parts—a question or incomplete statement (called the *stem*) followed by several choices. The student's task is to choose the one correct response from the choices. All incorrect choices are called *distractors*. Distractors are intended to encourage students to think a little harder about the task.

Sample of multiple-choice task

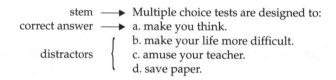

```
        stem ──▶ Multiple choice tests are designed to:
correct answer ──▶ a. make you think.
                    ⎧ b. make your life more difficult.
      distractors  ⎨ c. amuse your teacher.
                    ⎩ d. save paper.
```

Discuss basic strategies for completing multiple-choice tasks, including the following:

- Glance over the test. Get a feel for the type of questions and estimate how long it will take you complete the test. Pace yourself—most tests give you about one minute per multiple-choice item.
- Read all directions carefully. Although most tasks ask you to choose one best answer, some tests require that you choose more than one answer.
- Read the question or statement and try to answer or complete it **before** looking at the possible answers. Then, look over the answers and see if your answer is there. If it is, mark it and move on to the next question.
- If you don't know the answer right away, check out each possibility by reading the beginning of the question with each of the potential answers. This will give you a better ideas of which response sounds right.
- Read **all** choices before deciding on an answer.
- Look for any answers that are obviously wrong and cross them out. Choose the best answer from the remaining answers.
- When in doubt, make a smart guess and stick with it.
- Use information included in statements and questions to help you answer other questions. This may be especially helpful when you have completed the entire test and are going back to review your answers.

True/False Tasks

Make sure students know these strategies for true/false tasks:

- Read the statement slowly and carefully, word by word. If any part of the statement is false, the entire statement is false.
- Pay close attention to qualifying words, such as "all," "most," "never," "usually," and "always."

Long-answer Tasks

Teach students how to do a "splashdown" or "brain-drain" just before starting a longer assessment task, such as an essay question. Encourage them to take two minutes, using scrap paper or the bottom of the test paper, to jot down keywords, memory triggers, dates, names, formulas, and other special information they can use in completing the assessment task. This can serve as their outline. Some students may find it helpful to take the splashdown information and organize it into a web or list.

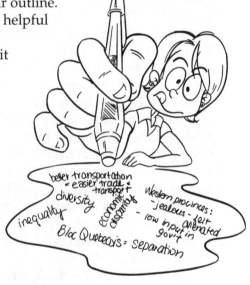

Share other strategies for completing essay responses such as the following:

- If there is more than one essay question, begin with the easy one first.
- Restate the question in your own words to make sure you really understand it. If you are unsure, read the question again.
- Use keywords or a web to outline your answer before your start writing. Put your ideas in order.
- If your answer is long, write an introduction sentence restating the question and write a conclusion summarizing the key points in your answer.

Practising Assessment Tasks

Students need opportunities at each grade level to practise with sample assessment formats and tasks. Students can work through sample tests with partners or in small groups, discussing correct answers and reasons why they choose one answer over another. Create opportunities for students to hear each other talk about their reasoning and test-taking strategies so they are better able to identify the most effective practices.

Managing Test Stress

Some students may be anxious before a test because they are worried about forgetting all they studied, getting a low score, or not being able to complete the test within the time limit. Fears such as these can become barriers to thinking and performance. Some students will need help identifying and eliminating sources of anxiety so they are able to concentrate on showing what they know rather than worrying about what they don't know.

Identifying Stress

Use Student Tool #7: How Do You Feel about Tests? (page 119) to help students identify their feelings and attitudes about tests. Students could work through the questionnaire on their own, with a partner, or as part of class discussion. Completing the tool will help students examine their attitudes and will encourage them to identify supports and strategies that can help them improve, not only their attitude toward testing, but their actual test performance. By sharing ideas about successful study strategies and ways to manage feelings, individual students can gain a new understanding and appreciation for what they can do to improve their own learning and school success.

Observe students closely to identify signs of anxiety before tests are given. Consider whether the anxiety may be a student's personal characteristic or is a temporary reaction to performing and being evaluated. Sometimes the anxiety is related to the subject area being tested; some students get nervous only during tests on particular subject areas. Confidence may also fluctuate based on the material being assessed; some students are more comfortable with certain topics or types of material. Consider how adults could be contributing to students' feelings of anxiety. Adults who exhibit high levels of test anxiety can transfer those feelings to students.

Fear of failure is the single most common cause of test anxiety. Students need to know that their test scores will not determine whether they pass or fail from one grade to the next. Low test scores should not be equated with punishment. Help individual students identify their specific fears about tests and why they might feel this way. This awareness is the first step toward developing strategies for overcoming fears and looking at each test as a challenge they are capable of handling.

Positive and Negative Stress

Teach students how to differentiate between positive and negative kinds of stress. Share information about different kinds of stress and discuss examples from everyday life.

- Negative stress occurs when you want to get away from an event or situation. It can be caused by the thought of anything that makes you uncomfortable. Anxiety is a feeling you have when you think there is something to dread or fear.

How Do You Feel about Tests?

Name: _____   Date:_____

1. How do you **feel** before tests?

_____

_____

2. What would you need to make **higher score** on tests?

_____

_____

3. What has **frustrated** you about a test?

_____

_____

4. What have you **enjoyed** doing on a test?

_____

_____

5. How could your **parents** help you prepare better for a test?

_____

_____

6. How could your **teachers** help you prepare better for a test?

_____

_____

7. What would make you feel more **comfortable** during tests?

_____

_____

8. How would you like to **celebrate** when you've finished a test?

_____

_____

- If you are afraid of tests, your nervous system can respond to tests in the same way it responds to the fear of an approaching wild animal! It goes into an emergency response mode, notifying the body to produce adrenaline so you can protect yourself by either fight or flight. Thinking and creativity can be blocked because your mind is so busy making plans for how to protect yourself. This is not a good kind of stress, it can prevent you from doing well on tests and you need to control it.
- On the other hand, good stress can actually help you do better on a test. Good stress causes adrenaline to produce a surge of energy, and you feel the excitement of a challenge. This revved-up feeling enhances performance. A few nervous jitters may be a healthy way for your body to let you know this test is important and that you are concerned that you will do your best. So it is actually okay to be a little nervous—this feeling can even get you a little extra energy. Athletes and other performers often say that a little anxiety before an important event is a definite advantage, that it focuses energy and sharpens thinking.

Stress-management Strategies

To help students develop strategies for managing stress, first encourage them to identify and verbalize their specific fears, such as

- "I will forget information."
- "I will not finish the test."
- "I won't make the mark my parents want me to."
- "The test will ask questions I don't know."

As a class, brainstorm strategies for coping with each example of a test fear. Discuss how, the more prepared student are for tests, the less anxious they are likely to be.

Teach students exercises specifically designed to reduce anxiety. For example, they could try a re-focusing exercise:

1. Close your eyes.
2. Breathe deeply and slowly ten times.
3. Think about relaxing your hands.
4. Say to yourself, "I can do this test one question at a time."

Encourage students to develop their own stress-busting strategies.

Self-talk

Confidence is a direct reflection of past experiences. It is the trust students have in their own abilities. This self-trust and confidence is a major key to approaching tests in a relaxed, controlled way (Chapman and King, page 76).

Negative Self-talk

Students who lack self-confidence may display various behaviors. They may cheat because they want to have good scores and do not want to disappoint their parents and teachers. Other students may appear to have an "I don't care" attitude. This, too, may be a cover-up for low self-confidence (Chapman and King, page 76).

Many students approach tests with negative messages playing in their heads. Help students become aware of the self-talk they are using by brainstorming examples of self-talk that could interfere with test success. For example:

- "I don't do well on tests."
- "This is too hard."
- "I never get the right answers."

Positive Self-talk

Have students to brainstorm lists of positive self-talk they can use, such as the following statements:

- "Learning and remembering is easy for me."
- "I have a good brain. I can do this."
- "This is my chance to show what I know."

Encourage students to develop positive self-talk statements that are first person singular—"Focus *my* attention" rather than "Focus *your* attention"—and are stated in the present tense. Students can use these statements to

- help define problems
- get started on difficult tasks
- guide themselves through processes
- cope with challenges or emotions
- provide themselves with encouragement and positive reinforcement

Self-talk can help students focus, follow-through, and finish a task.

Focus	Follow-through	Finish
"I have about ten minutes to do this part of the test. I can do this. I'm a smart test taker."	"I just need to keep going. I'm not sure of this question so I'll mark it with a star and come back to it at the end."	"Just two more questions. Now I'll go back and make sure I have an answer for every question."

Students can make self-talk cards and tape them to their desks to remind them of words they can use to encourage themselves. Remind students to use positive self-talk at different points throughout the school day, not only during testing situations. Positive self-talk can not only help students improve academically, it can help them break the negative self-talk cycles that might be contributing to feelings of panic, stress, and an unwillingness to try.

Dealing with Distractions

Distractions are interruptions that divert attention and focus from the task at hand. They are aspects of the physical environment—such as odd noises, smells, or lights—that get in the way of thinking and academic performance. People in the environment can also be a source of distraction when they talk or move around. Other distractions are internal, such as fatigue, sleepiness, hunger, thirst, anxiety, physical discomfort or pain, and preoccupation with other thoughts and events in your life. Many of these factors can be controlled, and students can learn to manage and overcome many of these distractions.

Different students are distracted by different things. For example, some people find music playing while they are working helps them concentrate better. Others need quiet while they work. It is difficult to satisfy the personal needs of all students all the time. Knowing what the common distractions might be can help teachers (and students) avoid and minimize problems on the day of the test.

There are some obvious things the teacher can do to minimize distractions, such as closing the classroom door or making sure that there are no announcements over the public address system during the test time, but some distractions are inevitable. Students need to learn how to concentrate and stay focused when distractions occur during tests and other learning activities. They also need to know how to

- re-focus and return quickly to the task,
- hold their place on a test, and
- react in various distracting situations.

Create opportunities for students to build their concentration skills through practice. During targeted classroom activities, challenge students to concentrate despite distractions you make intentionally. Use your acting skills to shuffle papers dramatically or sneeze loudly several times in a row. Discuss strategies for different scenarios.

What if ...

- someone whispers to you?
- there is a knock on the door?
- there is a noise in the hallway?
- your pencil breaks?
- you need to go to the washroom?
- you lose your place on the test?
- you have a question about a word on the test?
- you don't feel well?

Encourage students to share ideas and strategies for how they would handle each of the distracting situations you have proposed.

Parent Involvement

Students of all ages benefit from their parents' support and encouragement. Parents are a student's most influential teachers. When parents are actively involved in their children's learning, students' positive attitudes and behaviors increase, and they achieve more during class and perform better on assessment tasks. Meaningful parent involvement also leads to increased parent satisfaction with school programming.

It is vital to communicate with parents about important school activities as well as how their children are doing academically. Receiving communication from parents is equally important. A questionnaire such as Home Tool #3: Rate your Child's Test Smarts (page 126), used at the beginning of the school year, can get parents' help identifying their children's work habits and attitudes towards tests. Use the information from the questionnaire to help you better understand each student's needs so you can tailor instruction and ensure all students become smart test-takers.

The way parents talk about tests can influence children's attitudes and general self-confidence. As parents discuss test scores and test-taking experiences with their children, and even with other parents, friends, and relatives, their anxiety can be passed on. It is important that both parents and teachers maintain a positive tone that is supportive, is encouraging, and builds confidence. Share information and strategies with parents on how to support their children's success on tests. Send home Home Tool #4: Ten Tips for Building your Child's Test Smarts (page 127), or make it part of a discussion at a school council meeting or other school-hosted event.

Knowing that their children are learning new information and new skills can be a source of pride and satisfaction for parents. When parents share these feelings with their children, the whole family will begin to see tests as positive opportunities for students to show what they know. With this kind of positive perception, children are more likely to approach test taking with anticipation, enthusiasm, and confidence. Use Home Tool #5: Parent Reflection Guide (Chapter 8 page 139) to share strategies for discussing and supporting a child's test successes.

Class newsletters, school bulletin boards, and other handouts are also useful communication tools for sharing ideas with parents. The Home Tools on pages 109, 114, and 127 all offer practical advice that parents can use to help their children develop better study skills and test-taking strategies.

Consider hosting an information session for parents on how to help children build their test smarts. For ideas on what might work at your school, have a look at the sample notice and agenda for a parent information night that follow. This event was developed by a mid-size elementary school and became so popular with parents that it became an annual event.

Sample notice for a parent information session	Working together—for student achievement

How to help your children do their best on tests

An information night for parents and Grade 5 students of Duggan School

A. Why we do tests
B. Concerns parents might have about tests
C. What tests will look like
D. Ideas for reviewing at home
E. Smart test-taking tips
F. Ideas for building your child's test smarts

Wednesday, September 11, 20—
7 p.m. to 8 p.m.
Duggan School Library

*Students are encouraged to join their parents
for this information session.*

Sample agenda for a parent information session	Welcome and introductions

A. Why we do tests
Discuss the positive ways tests can be used. For example:
We use information from tests as a positive tool to improve our classroom instruction practices so student learning is enhanced. Test data is feedback to students, parents, and teachers about what individual students are learning—tests create opportunities to gather evidence and celebrate!

Data from tests can also provide information about
- what students are learning and understanding
- what skills and concepts individuals and groups of students need more instruction and practice with
- what areas of instruction are working well (so we can keep doing it!)
- areas of instruction we need to keep working on
- what schools need to do to better support student learning

B. Concerns parents might have about tests
Consider the common questions parents might have about tests and be prepared to answer them. For example:
- How do you make sure tests are fair for individual children?
  "We align test questions with grade-level learning outcomes and offer support for students who may have difficulty reading the test or recording answers."
- Do they cause stress for children?
  "Yes, but it's the good kind of stress! We also talk about test anxiety in class and show children practical ways they can handle these feelings."
- Do they tell us what we need to know?
  "Not everything, but they are one part of the picture. There are many other ways we assess student learning including…"
- How does the school use test results?
  "We use them to encourage learners, celebrate our successes, and improve our teaching practices."

C. What the tests will look like

Provide overview of types of questions and show sample tasks on the overhead. Discuss a specific learner outcome and then show a sample question. Have some fun with the questions—do the parents know the answers? Encourage students to discuss the answers and show their thinking about specific test items.

D. Ideas for reviewing at home

Distribute course outlines or website addresses so parents have access to specific learner outcomes for core subject areas.

Distribute Home Tool #1: Ten Smart Study Tricks (page 109). Choose three study tricks and have students demonstrate how to use them with a specific passage of information. Introduce a sample study plan for three nights and encourage

- short and frequent reviews (from 15 to 60 minutes per day)
- over learning
- reading aloud and discussing information in your own words.

E. Smart test-taking tips

Distribute Student Tool #5: Tips on Test Taking (page 113). Review on overhead or have students review with their parents. Time permitting, introduce and model a specific test-taking strategy such as splashdown or SCORER.

F. Ideas for building your child's test smarts

Distribute Home Tool #4: Ten Tips for Building your Child's Test Smarts (page 127) and review ideas. Discuss the importance of maintaining a positive attitude and using encouraging words. Ask for additional ideas from participating parents and record on overhead.

Review schedule of tests for the school year.

Rate your Child's Test Smarts

Child's name_____

Date _____

Read each statement and check *yes* or *not yet*.

My child

1. approaches tests confidently and positively.   ❏ yes   ❏ not yet

2. understands the basic purpose of tests.   ❏ yes   ❏ not yet

3. talks to me about each test.   ❏ yes   ❏ not yet

4. asks for assistance when studying for tests.   ❏ yes   ❏ not yet

5. prepares for tests as part of the regular homework routine two or three nights before the test.   ❏ yes   ❏ not yet

6. brings home the necessary information and material to review for a test.   ❏ yes   ❏ not yet

7. understands what material will be on a each test.   ❏ yes   ❏ not yet

8. demonstrates a willingness and interest in preparing for tests.   ❏ yes   ❏ not yet

9. knows three or four ways to review concepts and skills.   ❏ yes   ❏ not yet

10. can effectively review for tests with a classmate.   ❏ yes   ❏ not yet

11. reviews completed tests so he or she can do better next time.   ❏ yes   ❏ not yet

12. celebrates his or her test successes.   ❏ yes   ❏ not yet

Ten Tips for Building

your Child's Test Smarts

1. Make time in your family's busy schedule to review with your child for 15 to 60 minutes a night for three or four nights before a major test.

2. Look for interesting and fun ways to review information and help your child practise new skills he or her she is learning in school.

3. Offer encouraging words, such as

   "Give the test your best."

   "This test is a great opportunity to show how much you know."

   "You will do a great job."

4. Talk about how a little stress can be a good thing—it can encourage people to do their best. Share strategies for handling stress such as breathing deeply and using positive self-talk.

5. Encourage your child to choose clothes and pack his or her knapsack the night before to ensure a more relaxed, less rushed start the next morning.

6. Ensure your child has a good night's sleep the night before the test.

7. Prepare a healthy breakfast for your child on the morning of the test.

8. Ensure your child arrives at school on time and has any supplies needed on the day of the test.

9. Plan a special family activity to celebrate your child doing his or her best on a test.

10. Review the scored test with your child and identify what he or she did well. Look at mistakes as opportunities for learning and setting new goals.

7

Smart Test Time

There are a number of strategies that teachers can use on the day of the test to help students perform more successfully. Consider the many factors that make a difference to the comfort level of your students. Look for ways to focus their attention and build their confidence and motivation including:

- modifying the physical classroom set-up
- giving pep talks
- helping students manage their time
- ending on a positive note
- ensuring all students finish tests, and
- making provisions for students with special learning needs.

Classroom Set-up

Even the way desks are arranged and supplies are made available can affect students' test performance. Depending on the physical set-up of the classroom, it may be necessary to re-configure the classroom furniture on the day of the test. If desks are clustered together to facilitate group work, you may need to rearrange them so that students will clearly understand that test taking is different from regular class work. In a testing situation, students must work alone to show what they know; it's not a time to interact with others.

Plan how you will assign seating so each child will have optimum space and privacy to concentrate on the test. Take advantage of empty desks, tables, or other activity areas in the classroom. Consider having students make paper name tents the day before the test so you can assign test-writing places before students arrive on the day of the test. Having students participate in the rearrangement of the room can create additional opportunities to discuss and reinforce how test taking situations differ from other types of learning activities.

Sample of a name tent

Have sharpened pencils, extra erasers, and other supplies available for individual students to borrow on an as-needed basis. Students need to concentrate on maintaining a positive attitude and giving their best effort during the test, not worry about finding a pencil or fret over a missing ruler. If it is part of the class routine, ensure freshly filled water bottles are available on each desk.

Use student-created signs to let others students and staff in the school know that the class will be hard at work on a test and will appreciate quiet and no interruptions. Keep the message positive and upbeat. Hang one sign on the outside of the classroom door and post the other on the front board. Discuss the message on the sign and encourage students to develop additional messages and signs for future test-taking.

Samples of test-in-progress signs

Doing our best on a test!

Quiet please: brains at work.

Test-in-progress: We're showing what we know.

When students are seated and have their supplies assembled on their work areas, pass out test papers face down on the desk and ask students to wait for a signal to turn over the test and begin.

Giving Pep Talks

A positive attitude can go a long way to improving test performance. Take a few minutes before the test begins to deliver the message that this test is based on all the hard work students have been doing over the last few weeks or months. Explain that the test contains questions and tasks that all of the students in class should be able to do successfully because they have had lots of practice in class. Prepare them for the fact that some questions might look new because information and ideas can be presented in many ways and with many different words. Emphasize that this test is an opportunity for students to really think about all the things they are learning and to show how well they understand these new skills and concepts.

To help students develop an understanding of how a positive attitude can effect test success, consider using Student Tool #8: Assess your Test-smart Attitude (page 131) before a major test.

During the pep talk, model positive self-talk (see Chapter 6) and invite individual students to share examples of phrases they can use to encourage themselves during the test.

Also remind students to use any test-taking strategies they may have learned, such as splashdowns (see Chapter 6) or SCORER (see Home Tool #2, page 114). It may be helpful to have posters with step-by-step directions for these strategies displayed prominently in the classroom or on cards on individual desks.

Discuss basic rules for test-taking. For example:

- Do your best thinking and writing.
- Stay in your area.
- Work quietly and let others do their own work.

Decide on whether or not students will be allowed to ask for reading assistance with test questions. With younger students, it may be necessary. When students ask for assistance, encourage them to first tell you what they think the question is asking and then verify or correct their interpretation. Unless a test is intended to assess specific reading skills, students' success on the test should not be adversely affected by their reading skills (or lack of reading skills).

Helping Students Manage their Time

Students' ability to manage their time can affect test performance. Discuss timelines with students, and write these times on the board. Set both a minimum and maximum time, but emphasize that everyone will have the time they need to finish the test. Specify what students should do if they finish the test before the allotted time. For example, use instructions like this:

- "This test will take about one hour to complete. Some people might be finished before others, but everyone must remain at your desk for the first half hour."
- "When you are finished your test look it over to make sure you have answered each question. There should be no blanks!"
- "Read over each question and think about what the question is asking you to do. If your answer is very short, see if you can add more information. Ask yourself, 'Am I showing all I know? Will the teacher understand my answer?'"
- "When you've finished your test, raise your hand so the teacher can pick up your paper. Then you may go quietly to the reading corner and read a book on the carpet."

For longer tests, it may be helpful to provide prompts at regular intervals throughout the test, noting how much time is left and approximately how may questions students should have completed. Record this information on the board

Assess your Test-smart Attitude

Name: _____   Date:_____

1. I feel good about taking tests.

   ❒ always   ❒ often   ❒ sometimes   ❒ rarely or never

2. I know how to study for a test.

   ❒ always   ❒ often   ❒ sometimes   ❒ rarely or never

3. I always score high on tests.

   ❒ always   ❒ often   ❒ sometimes   ❒ rarely or never

4. I bring the supplies I need.

   ❒ always   ❒ often   ❒ sometimes   ❒ rarely or never

5. I feel confident when I am writing tests.

   ❒ always   ❒ often   ❒ sometimes   ❒ rarely or never

6. It is easy for me to remember information I have learned in class.

   ❒ always   ❒ often   ❒ sometimes   ❒ rarely or never

7. I can concentrate on the test.

   ❒ always   ❒ often   ❒ sometimes   ❒ rarely or never

8. I can finish tests within the time limit.

   ❒ always   ❒ often   ❒ sometimes   ❒ rarely or never

9. I use positive self-talk to encourage myself.

   ❒ always   ❒ often   ❒ sometimes   ❒ rarely or never

so students can gauge their own progress. It may be helpful to walk around the room and informally check on student progress so you can better predict where the majority of students need to be in order to complete the test within the timelines.

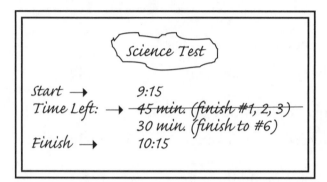

As individual students hand in their test papers, skim quickly over them as time permits. If there are missing answers or an answer is obviously incomplete, point it out and encourage students to give it another try and really "show what they know." As students become more experienced test takers you can gradually fade out this level of support. For example, young students might need a specific incomplete question identified whereas more mature students might need a simple prompt, such as "Check your answers—there is something missing."

Ending on a Positive Note

It's important to end the test-taking experience on a positive note in order to create positive and high expectations for future experiences. Develop a class ritual for the end of a test-taking session, such as having students give themselves a round of applause, a standing ovation, or a class cheer. It also might be good time for a favorite class game or shared story.

Ensure All Students Finish the Test

It's essential that all students finish the test. For those few students who may need extra time, arrange for them to work on the test outside the classroom at some point during the school day. Decide if working through recess would be a motivation or a deterrent to an individual student. Older students who require extra time may be more willing to work through recess or the noon hour when they realize this type of accommodation lets them finish the test successfully without missing out on any class activities.

It's especially important that younger students successfully complete major tests, even if finishing means getting extra time and support from the teacher. This is a short-term investment for long-term gains; a successfully completed test goes a long way toward helping students build their confidence for future test-taking experiences.

This short-term intervention can also be an opportunity for one-on-one coaching of test-taking skills. Identify the questions the student is struggling with and encourage the student to reflect on what the question is asking by putting it in his or her own words. If necessary, help the student rephrase the question and discuss what kinds of things the student needs to think about in order to answer the question or complete the assessment task successfully. If the student is temporarily discouraged or tired, it may be necessary for the teacher to record the answers and assure them that next time "You can write it down for yourself."

Older students sometimes develop negative coping skills during tests, including getting stuck on first questions and not using time effectively, passing in incomplete papers, and missing class on the day of scheduled tests. By ensuring students have positive experiences writing tests in the elementary grades, students are less likely to develop these negative ways of coping and are more likely to build strong study skills and effective test-taking habits.

Accommodating Students with Special Needs

Some students, particularly those with special needs, may require additional accommodations during test taking to ensure that they have a fair opportunity to demonstrate their learning. Accommodations could include assistance with reading the questions or recording the answers, and adjustments to time or writing requirements. Some accommodations may take the form of adaptive or assistive technology or individualized prompts. A small number of students may need the actual content of the test adjusted to better align with their developmental levels, learning styles, and individualized education goals.

Extra Time

Some students may consistently require additional time to prepare for and write tests. Older children may be able to use recesses or lunch time to make up this time, but younger children will have to be accommodated during class time. Part of this accommodation includes helping children set goals for how long they will take to complete a task, self-monitor how long they actually take, and work to improve their time management skills so they can use test time more effectively and not miss out on other learning activities.

Reading Difficulties

For students with reading difficulties, extra assistance can be as simple as answering questions about a word or phrase on the test. Students with more severe reading difficulties may need an adult to read the questions one at a time to them.

If the reading difficulties are quite severe, consider how assistive technology could be used to increase an individual student's reading independence. Some students may benefit from an audio recording of the test. Other students might benefit from test-reading software programs, in which the text of the test is scanned and displayed on a computer screen while a computerized voice reads the test. These types of programs generally allow students to adjust reading speed, voice quality, and size of print. They often have additional features that allow students to reread text. Some programs have built-in dictionaries so students can check the meaning of unfamiliar words. If the computer is located in the classroom, students using these programs will need to use headsets so the rest of the class is not disturbed.

Spelling Difficulties

If spelling is a major challenge for an individual student, using an electronic spell-check or working directly on a word processor may be helpful. Younger student can be encouraged to refer to word-wall words, individual word banks, or personal dictionaries, if they are part of the regular classroom routine. Students should be assured that, unless the test is an actual test of spelling words, misspellings should not adversely affect their mark. For students with weak spelling skills, it might also be fair to ask them to clarify written answers that are difficult to decipher or understand.

Writing Difficulties

Some students will need assistance recording answers on tests. Assistance could be as simple as the teacher supplying requested words or phrases on a sticky note for students to copy onto the test sheet. In some cases, the teacher, a teacher assistant, or a classroom volunteer may have to record the answers for individual students.

For older students experiencing severe writing difficulties, a voice-generated software program may be helpful. Any assistive technology used in test-taking situations should be part of the student's daily classroom program. For any technology to be helpful, students will need initial instruction and opportunities for guided and independent practice.

In some cases it may be necessary to adjust writing requirements on an individual student basis. For example, the general expectation might be to answer questions in complete sentences, but individual students with writing difficulties might be allowed to answer with keywords or phrases without losing marks. The actual length of a response can also be modified; for example, individual students might be asked to give three factors instead of the standard five.

Differentiating Content

Students with special needs who have an individualized education plan and who need curriculum modifications may require individualized test questions and procedures.

8

Reporting and Using Test Results

Test results can provide teachers with rich information for improving instruction and better meeting the needs of students, both individually and collectively. But test data can also be valuable to students and parents. It can provide students with a new understanding of what and how they are learning, and it can give parents a better understanding of how they can support and motivate their children to become better learners.

Creating smart tests and communicating results effectively demonstrates your commitment to teaching students how to be better thinkers and more active learners. It is tangible evidence that you value what and how students learn.

Student Self-reflection

Once tests have been scored and shared with students, they need opportunities to reflect on what the results mean. When students go through their own tests and identify concepts that they understood well, they become more confident and motivated about their own learning. This kind of review can help them see how effort contributes to learning—and a good test score. They begin to realize that their marks are not simply a result of good or bad luck, but are a result of effective preparation, persistent commitment, and hard work.

As well as identifying areas of strength, test results can identify areas that need improvement. Students can use this information to set goals and develop action plans for improving their learning. Student Tool # 9: Thinking about My Test (page 137) invites students to reflect on how they did on a test and identify ways they can improve their performance on future tests. Consider having students complete a reflection guide in preparation for sharing their test results with parents.

Thinking about My Test

Name: _____   Date:_____

Tests are one of the many ways to find out what I know and understand about a topic.

My mark on the _____ test was _____.

This **mark** tells me

_____

_____

_____

I did well on the following **questions**:

_____

_____

_____

I was **successful** on these questions because

_____

_____

_____

To be **even more successful** on future tests I need to

_____

_____

_____

My **teachers and parents** can help me improve my learning by

_____

_____

_____

Sharing Test Results

Sharing Results with Parents

Sending tests home for parents to sign is a common practice. The primary intent is to inform parents of their child's progress. It is also assumed that parents and children will discuss the test results. To encourage this important parent–child dialogue, consider providing structured activities such as Home Tool #5: Parent Reflection Guide (page 139).

This type of feedback form can enhance communication between parents and children, and also between teachers and parents. Reflection guides create opportunities for parents to see *what* students are learning as well as *how well* they are doing.

Students should make corrections before they share their test results with parents. This practice boosts students' confidence because they will be able to demonstrate to parents that, although they may have written a wrong answer at the time of the test, they now know the correct response.

Learning Conferences

Another effective way of communicating student learning is through parent–teacher–student learning conferences. A marked and corrected test can provide a representative and informative sample of student learning. It may include tasks in which students were successful, as well as those demonstrating areas of difficulty.

Highlighting areas of strength at the beginning of the conference will help both parents and students feel more at ease and encourage a more open and constructive dialogue.

Parents will also want to know about areas needing improvement so they can better support their child's learning. For students experiencing a great deal of difficulty, select only one or two areas of focus, leaving discussion about the other areas in need of improvement for a later date. A lengthy list of problems will be discouraging for everyone. When students are active participants in the conference, their input into how to improve can be very valuable. When included in the discussion, they may be more willing to set goals and make commitments, particularly when they are encouraged to set short-term goals that are attainable and meaningful to them.

Progress Reports

Progress reporting can take many forms, from lists of numerical scores to individualized comments. Using test results to support comments on report card puts the focus on skills and concepts, and provides tangible evidence of how students are performing.

Test scores do not tell the whole story; parents need to know what the results mean in the context of a unit of study or a set of skills. Use test results to provide specific information that illustrates students' strengths and areas of need; for

Parent Reflection Guide

Student name _____

Test _____

I see that you understand the following skills and concepts:

_____

_____

_____

I see that you need to improve in the following areas:

_____

_____

_____

After reviewing this test with you, I would like you to (check all that apply)

❏ learn more about _____.

❏ keep up the good work.

❏ practise _____ more at home.

Parent signature _____ Date _____

example, "The Social Studies unit test shows that Tara clearly understands
_____ but has a limited understanding of _____."

As well as identifying strengths and needs, test results can also be used to identify areas of focus for the next term or school year. These types of challenge
statements are even more effective if they have student input, reflected in such
statements such as "This term Daniel's essay questions on tests tended to lack
detail and organization. He has committed to improving these two writing skills
in the new term."

Why Share Test Results?

Taking the time to communicate what test results mean helps students and
parents see that tests are another opportunity to learn, rather than a simple culmi-
nation of a unit. Making the follow up to tests memorable, positive, and
meaningful creates opportunities for students to take more responsibility for their
own learning and engage more fully in classroom instruction. It also creates
opportunities for parents to know more about what and how their children are
learning so they are better able to support their children's learning and success in
school.

Bibliography

Alberta Assessment Consortium. *Smerging Data: More Than Just Number Crunching.* Edmonton, AB: Alberta Assessment Consortium, 2001

Alberta Education. *The Parent Advantage: Helping Children Become More Successful Learners at Home and School, Grades 1–9.* Edmonton, AB: Alberta Education, 1998

Alberta Learning. *Make School Work for You: A Resource for Junior and Senior High Students Who Want to be More Successful Learners.* Edmonton, AB: Alberta Learning, 2001

Antaya-Moore, Dana and Catherine Walker. *Smart Learning: Strategies for Parents, Teachers and Kids.* Edmonton, AB: Smart Learning, 1996

Ban, John R. *Parents Assuring Students Success: Achievement Made Easy by Learning Together,* second edition. Bloomington, IN: National Educational Service, 2000

Brown. R. "Testing and Thoughtfulness" in *Educational Leadership,* April 1989, pp. 113–115

Burke, Kay. *The Mindful School: How to Assess Authentic Learning,* third edition. Arlington Heights, IL.: SkyLight Professional Development, 1999

Cecil, Nancy Lee. *The Art of Inquiry: Questioning Strategies for K–6 Classrooms.* Winnipeg, MN: Peguis Publishers, 1995

Centre for Research in Applied Measurement and Evaluation. *Principles for Fair Student Assessment Practices for Education in Canada.* Edmonton, AB: Joint Advisory Committee, Centre for Research in Applied Measurement and Evaluation, University of Alberta, 1993

Chapman, Carolyn and Rita King. *Test Success in the Brain-compatible Classroom.* Tucson, AZ.: Zephyr Press, 2000

Dodge, Judith. *The Study Skills Handbook: More Than 75 Strategies for Better Learning.* New York, NY: Scholastic Inc., 1994

Edmonton Public Schools. *Thinking Tools for Kids: Practical Organizers.* Edmonton, AB: Edmonton Public Schools, Resource Development Services, 1999

—— *Think Again: Practical Organizers for Grades 6–10.* Edmonton, AB: Edmonton Public Schools, Resource Development Services, 2003

Fogarty, Robin. *How to Raise Test Scores.* Arlington Heights, IL: SkyLight Professional Development, 1999

Guskey, T.R. "How Classroom Assessments Improve Learning" in *Educational Leadership,* (60) 5, 2003, pp. 7–16.

Manning, Brenda H. "Self-talk and Learning" in *Teaching K–8.* April 1990, pp. 56–58

Marzano, Robert, *Transforming Classroom Grading.* Alexandria, VA: Association for Supervision and Curriculum Development , 2000

Murphy, Deborah A. et al. *Exceptions: A Handbook of Inclusive Activities for Teachers of Students at Grades 6–12 with Mild Disabilities*. Longmont, CO: Sopris West, 1988–1994

O'Connor, Ken. *The Mindful School: How to Grade for Learning*. Arlington Heights, IL: SkyLight Professional Development, 1999

Politano, Colleen and Joy Paquin. *Brain-based Learning with Class*. Winnipeg, MB: Portage & Main Press, 2000

Popham, W.J. "The Seductive Allure of Data" in *Educational Leadership*, (60) 5, 2003, pp. 48–51.

Rudner, L. and W. Schafer (2002) *What Teachers Need to Know About Assessment*. Washington, DC: National Education Association. From the free online version. Accessed November 2002 at http://ericae.net/books/nea/teachers.pdf

Schumm, Jeanne Shay. *School Power: Study Skill Strategies for Succeeding in School* revised and updated edition. Minneapolis, MN: Free Spirit Publishing Inc., 2001

Stevens, B.A. and A. Tollafield. "Creating Comfortable and Productive Parent/Teacher Conferences" in *Phi Delta Kappan*.(84) 7, 2003, pp. 521–524

Stiggins, Richard. *Student-Centered Classroom Assessment*, second edition. Upper Saddle River, NJ: Prentice-Hall, 1997

Stiggins, Richard and Tanis Knight. *But Are They Learning? A Commonsense Parents' Guide to Assessment and Grading in Schools*. Portland, OR: Assessment Training Institute, Inc. 1998

Taylor, Kathe and Sherry Walton. "Testing Pitfalls (and how to help kids avoid them)" in *Scholastic Instructor*, Vol. III, No. 2, October 2001, pp. 26, 84–85.

Wahlberg, H.J., G.D. Haertel and S.Gerlach-Downie. *Assessment Reform: Challenges and Opportunities*. Bloomington, Indiana: Phi Delta Kappa Educational Foundation, 1994